D-DAY LANDINGS

A TRAVEL GUIDE TO NORMANDY'S BEACHES & BATTLEGROUNDS

SITES • MUSEUMS • MEMORIALS

MARY ANNE EVANS
ALASTAIR McKENZIE

www.bradtguides.com

Bradt Guides Ltd, UK
The Globe Pequot Press Inc, USA

Bradt GUIDES
TRAVEL TAKEN SERIOUSLY

First published March 2024
Bradt Guides Ltd
31a High Street, Chesham, Buckinghamshire, HP5 1BW, England
www.bradtguides.com
Print edition published in the USA by The Globe Pequot Press Inc, PO Box 480,
Guilford, Connecticut 06437-0480

ISBN: 9781804691700

British Library Cataloguing in Publication Data
A catalogue record for this book is available from the British Library

Photographs © individual photographers and organisations credited beside
images & also from picture libraries credited as follows: Alamy.com (A);
Dreamstime.com (D); Shutterstock.com (S); Superstock.com (SS); US National
Archives and Records Administration (NARA)

Front cover Courseulles-sur-Mer Beach (John Potter/A)
Back cover, clockwise from top left The British Normandy Memorial (olrat/S); the
Higgins boat statue at the Utah Beach Landing Museum (olrat/S); Longues-sur-
Mer Battery (Matthew Troke/D)
Title page, clockwise from top left The Normandy American Cemetery at Colleville-
sur-Mer (SS); 29th Infantry Division memorial at Vierville-sur-Mer (SS);
Airborne Museum in Sainte-Mère-Église (Airborne Museum)
Part openers Page 1: Bomber over Normandy on 8 June 1944 (Everett Collection/S);
page 13: Canadian troops storm Juno Beach (Wikimedia Commons); page 105: a
tank in the bocage in July 1944 (Everett Collection/S)

Maps David McCutcheon FBCart.S. FRGS

Typeset by Ian Spick, Bradt Guides
Production managed by Zenith Media; printed in the UK
Digital conversion by www.dataworks.co.in

AUTHORS

Mary Anne Evans is an established guidebook writer, journalist and editor. She is a member of the British Guild of Travel Writers and has written about destinations in Europe for numerous magazines and websites. An expert on France, she now runs her own specialist website, Mary Anne's France (w maryannesfrance.com).

Alastair McKenzie is a travel blogger and former national radio travel editor/presenter. He has been a member of the British Guild of Travel Writers for over two decades and now runs a specialist blog, Mechtraveller (w mechtraveller.com), which focuses on historic sites, battlefields, technical/military museums, and past and future transport systems.

ACKNOWLEDGEMENTS

We would like to thank Ben Collier (Normandy Tourism), Mathilde Lelandais (Coeur de Nacre Tourisme), Atout France (UK), DFDS Ferries, Pierre et Vacances, and Julie Verne (British Normandy Memorial).

DEDICATION

Australian squadron leader W W 'Bill' Blessing DFC DSO was a Mosquito pilot with RAF No 106 Squadron (Pathfinders). He was newly married to Corporal Pamela Birch – a WAAF stationed at Stanmore, and late mother to co-author Alastair McKenzie from her second marriage – when he was shot down by a German fighter over Caen on 7 July 1944. He is buried in the Commonwealth War Graves Commission cemetery at Douvres-la-Délivrande and remembered on column 141 at the British Normandy Memorial in Ver-sur-Mer.

This book is dedicated to him, and all those who died in Normandy in 1944.

Contents

LIST OF MAPS

KEY TO SYMBOLS

▨▨▨	Motorway	⑥	Memorial
▨▨▨	Main road	⬚	Cemetery
══	Secondary road	●	Other point of interest
══	Other road	●	City
⊷⊷	Railway	○	Town
✈	Airport	▨	Parachute drop zone
𝑖	Tourist information	▨	Urban area
⚔	Museum		Beach

Introduction

When the German Luftwaffe lost the Battle of Britain in 1940, and Operation Sealion – Germany's planned invasion of Britain – had to be called off, Hitler's mind was already turning to his great ambition: the conquest of Russia. He considered Sealion to be merely postponed, or that it might not have to happen at all if the British sued for peace. The Japanese attack on Pearl Harbor in December 1941 changed all that. When America came into the war, it opened up the real threat of an Allied land invasion of German-occupied western Europe. If this happened, Hitler would have to fight the war on two fronts. So, just seven days after Pearl Harbor, he ordered the building of coastal fortifications from the North Cape of Norway to the Spanish border – his 'Atlantic Wall'.

At the same time, the Allies were already starting work on the colossal and detailed plans needed to tackle such defences, using a new military doctrine of 'machines not men'. The Germans would be overwhelmed by machinery and munitions in devastating quantities. The logistics of transporting all this across the channel to launch such a seaborne invasion took 2½ years to draw together and set in motion.

When D-Day – the Allied landing operations at Normandy – eventually took place on the morning of 6 June 1944, an armada of more than 6,900 ships and 1,900 transport aircraft and gliders delivered 132,000 soldiers and their equipment to the beaches, and 23,000 airborne troops inland. These were under the protection of 200 shore bombardment ships and 9,500 attack aircraft. That was just D-Day itself, but the assault continued. Five divisions landed on D-Day; by 20 August there were 39 Allied divisions in Normandy. It was the largest seaborne invasion in history, undertaken by 15 allied nations – and 2024, the year of publication for this book – marked the 80th anniversary.

'D-Day' is often used in a broad context, shorthand for 'the invasion of Normandy'. Actually, it marks the intersection between two operations: Operation Neptune, the naval exercise of delivering millions of men and equipment to the beaches of Normandy, and Operation Overlord, which covered what they were to do when they got there – the Battle of Normandy.

We are taking a visitor's-eye view of those landing beaches and battlefields, both for those who want to explore independently and for those who want to plan where

WHAT'S IN A NAME?

The National World War II Museum in New Orleans, USA, says its most asked question is: 'What does the "D" in D-Day stand for?' Offered suggestions include Designated Day, Decision Day, Doomsday or even Death Day. It simply stands for 'Day' and is used as a point to count down from or up to, as in 'D+4' or 'D-14'. H-Hour is used the same way, and if you encounter a French book or signage on the subject, you'll see they call it Jour-J.

to go on a guided tour. The book is laid out geographically, with only a nod to historic chronology. The Battle of Normandy started neatly, with the Allies arriving on the coast, but quickly became confused as the battle developed. So the book is arranged in a lawnmower pattern: first working our way along the Normandy Coast from east to west, then returning the other way from Cherbourg, at the top of the Cotentin peninsula, through the areas around Saint-Lô, Falaise and finally Caen.

HOW TO USE THIS GUIDE

FINDING YOUR WAY Some sites, especially memorial stones, do not have street addresses and are not near obvious landmarks. The geocoding system What3Words (w what3words.com, or try the app) pinpoints locations to within a 3m square by allocating a unique combination of words, eg: /// hubcap.heaviest.cobble. These have been provided where locations are tricky to find.

ACCESSIBILITY Where sites and museums are wheelchair-accessible, we have indicated this by including & in the practical information. With a few exceptions, most memorials are to be found by the side of the road or in public squares/car parks, and so are wheelchair-accessible.

MILITARY TERMINOLOGY Army and navy units, equipment and other military words are used throughout. A glossary is provided (page 136).

FEEDBACK REQUEST

At Bradt Guides we're aware that guidebooks start to go out of date on the day they're published – and that you, our readers, are out there in the field doing research of your own. So why not tell us about your experiences? Contact us on ☎ 01753 893444 or e info@bradtguides.com. We will forward emails to the authors who may post updates on the Bradt website at w bradtguides.com/updates. Alternatively, you can add a review of the book to Amazon, or share your adventures with us on social:

BradtGuides, Mechtraveller & Maryannesfrance
BradtGuides & Mechtravel
BradtGuides

Part One

GENERAL INFORMATION

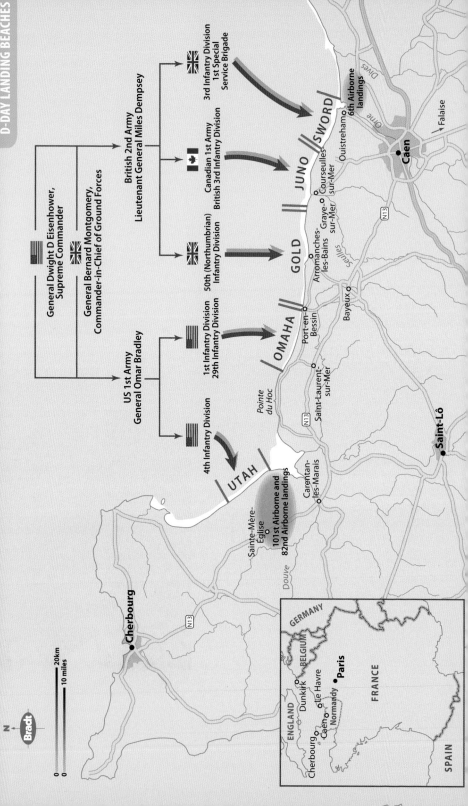

General Dwight D Eisenhower, Supreme Commander

General Bernard Montgomery, Commander-in-Chief of Ground Forces

US 1st Army
General Omar Bradley

British 2nd Army
Lieutenant General Miles Dempsey

4th Infantry Division

1st Infantry Division
29th Infantry Division

50th (Northumbrian)
Infantry Division

Canadian 1st Army
British 3rd Infantry Division

3rd Infantry Division
1st Special
Service Brigade

UTAH

OMAHA

GOLD

JUNO

SWORD

Sainte-Mère-
Église
101st Airborne and
82nd Airborne landings

Pointe
du Hoc

Carentan-
les-Marais

Saint-Laurent-
sur-Mer

Port-en-
Bessin

Arromanches-
les-Bains

Graye-
sur-Mer

Courseulles-
sur-Mer

Ouistreham

6th Airborne
landings

Bayeux

Saint-Lô

Caen

Falaise

Cherbourg

Douve

Seulles

Orne

Dives

N13

N13

N13

ENGLAND

Dunkirk

le Havre

Cherbourg

Caen

Normandy

GERMANY

BELGIUM

Paris

FRANCE

SPAIN

N

Bradt

0   20km
0   10 miles

1

Background Information

TIMELINE: WORLD WAR II

1 September 1939 Germany invades Poland; Great Britain and France declare war on Germany.

8 April 1940 Germany invades Norway, ending the 'Phoney War', a period of limited ground fighting in western Europe.

26 May–4 June 1940 British troops are evacuated at Dunkirk.

14 June 1940 The Nazis capture Paris; France signs an armistice with Germany on 22 June.

10 July–31 October 1940 The Battle of Britain between British and German air forces.

7 December 1941 Japan attacks Pearl Harbor; America enters the war.

1942–4 The war is focused in two areas: north Africa and the eastern front around Russia.

1943 The Allies begin planning a Normandy invasion: Operation Overlord.

6 June 1944 D-Day.

25 August 1944 Paris is liberated.

8 May 1945 Victory in Europe.

6 and 9 August 1945 The US drops atomic bombs on Hiroshima and Nagasaki.

15 August 1945 Japan surrenders; the war is over.

TIMELINE: OPERATION OVERLORD – THE BATTLE OF NORMANDY

[D-DAY] 6 JUNE 1944

00.15 British airborne troops land in the Orne Valley and US airborne troops land on the Cotentin Peninsula around Sainte-Mère-Église.

04.30 US Rangers arrive by sea at Pointe du Hoc.

06.30 Amphibious landings begin at Utah Beach (US) and Omaha Beach (US).

07.25 Amphibious landings begin at Gold (GB) and Sword (GB) beaches.

07.45 Amphibious landings begin at Juno Beach (CAN).

JUNE

[D+1] **7 June** The overall commander of the ground forces, General Bernard Montgomery of the British Army, steps ashore. British forces take Bayeux.

[D+4] **10 June** The British launch Operation Perch to try to capture Caen in a pincer movement, but are unsuccessful.

[D+8] **14 June** Charles de Gaulle – leader of the Free France government-in-exile, supporting the resistance against the Nazi occupation of France – visits. He goes to Bayeux to declare it the first Free French town.

[D+13] **19 June** A great storm wrecks the Mulberry A artificial harbour at Omaha Beach, and damages Mulberry B at Gold (Arromanches-les-Bains), hampering progress.

[D+20] **26 June** Under Operation Epsom, Allied forces begin their attempt to swing around Caen and capture the high ground south of the city.

[D+21] **27 June** Cherbourg is captured by US troops.

JULY

[D+32] **8 July** Anglo-Canadian forces renew attempts to capture Caen, after heavy naval and aerial bombardment.

[D+43] **19 July** British and Canadian forces finally capture Caen, while US forces liberate Saint-Lô.

[D+49] **25 July** Operation Cobra (page 114) sees US forces break out from the bottom of the Cotentin Peninsula and head towards Avranches and Brittany.

[D+51] **27 July** Périers is liberated.

AUGUST

[D+56] **1 August** Free of the difficult terrain in the bocage – areas of farmland divided by irrigation ditches, sunken lanes and tall hedges, which make up much of the peninsula – US forces split up at Avranches and race west into Brittany, south towards Rennes, and southeast towards Le Mans.

[D+59] **4 August** Hitler orders a counter-attack west towards Mortain and Avranches, inadvertently causing his troops to become encircled by US and Canadian forces.

[D+62] **7 August** The Canadian 1st Army advances south from around Caen in a bid to take Falaise. They capture the city on [D+72] 17 August.

[D+64] **9 August** US forces reach and liberate Le Mans, and then head north.

[D+76] **21 August** The trap is complete when Canadian and Polish troops meet up with the Americans and Free French at Chambois and Saint-Lambert-sur-Dives. German troops are surrounded in the so-called Falaise Pocket and are defeated.

2

Practical Information

GETTING THERE AND AROUND

The two major points of entry to the D-Day landing beaches are the ferry ports of Caen in the east and Cherbourg in the west, on the Cotentin Peninsula. Details of how to get from these to the different beaches and sites are included in each chapter.

BY AIR There are no airlines flying directly from the UK or the USA to Caen or Cherbourg. You can fly to Paris and travel on from there – the easiest, quickest way will be to take the train (page 7), although you can also take the bus (page 7) or hire a car (see below). You can fly from Paris to Caen in high season, but you have to change at Lyon, and other forms of transport will be quicker.

BY FERRY There are four main ports for travel **from the UK** to the Normandy D-Day landing beaches. The cheapest and quickest route (though the furthest from the Normandy beaches) is with **DFDS** (\ 0330 587 8787; w dfds.com; car ferry only; 4hrs), sailing from Newhaven to Dieppe. **Brittany Ferries** (\ 0330 159 7000; w brittany-ferries.co.uk) go from Portsmouth to Le Havre (7hrs), Ouistreham/Caen (7hrs) and Cherbourg (7hrs 45mins), or from Poole to Cherbourg (5½hrs).

From Ireland to Cherbourg, **Irish Ferries** (\ 0371 730 0400; w irishferries. com) sail from Dublin (approx 18½hrs); **Stenaline** (\ 0344 770 7070; w stenaline. co.uk) go from Rosslare (approx 15hrs 40mins); and Brittany Ferries also sail from Rosslare (approx 16hrs).

BY CAR Many of the World War II museums, memorials, battlefields and cemeteries are located in the countryside, so to visit them you really do need a car or a guide. If you've brought your car on the **ferry** to Cherbourg or Ouistreham (Caen), you will already be in the heart of Normandy. To drive to Ouistreham, the eastern gateway to the beaches, from the more distant ferry ports of Dieppe (200km; 2hrs 5mins) or Le Havre (105km; 1hr 20mins), you will mostly follow the A29 and the A13 (tolls from €18). There is also a fixed-charge toll to cross the Pont de Normandie over the River Seine, just south of Le Havre (€5.40). To reach Ouistreham from **Paris**, you'll take the A13 via Caen (252km; approx 3hrs; tolls approx €18). If you've driven from the UK via the **Channel Tunnel** (w eurotunnel. com) you'll enter France at Calais, from where it's 347km (approx 3hrs 30mins; tolls approx €30) to Ouistreham.

Renting a car in France The usual international car-hire firms operate out of the main towns like Caen and Cherbourg. We recommend travelling by train to Normandy, then hiring a car locally. Most car companies are at the ports, at train stations or near the centre of towns.

Driving in France Remember to drive on the right, give way to the right and take sufficient cash or credit cards to pay at French motorway tollbooths (*péages*). In France you must by law carry your driving licence, the car's registration document (a *carte grise*) and the car's insurance documents. You must also have a safety jacket and a warning triangle inside the car. If you've driven your car from the UK rather than hiring one locally, you must display a UK sticker in your car, not a GB sticker (unless your car's registration plate has UK on it). You must also have headlight beam deflectors. You can buy all the extra requirements at the UK port you're travelling from, onboard the ferry, or at the port you arrive at.

Within the Normandy region around the landing beaches, the two **roads** you will mainly use are: the N13, a *route nationale* major road and sometimes a dual carriageway; and the D514, a smaller road that runs mostly along the coast, connecting so many of the major locations. But it can be slow, particularly in the major summer holiday season.

There are **petrol stations** everywhere (though the autoroute petrol stations are pricier). **Parking** is mainly easy at the Normandy sites, but in the high season it's best to arrive either early or late at particularly popular places.

BY TRAIN If travelling **from the UK** by train, you will take the Eurostar (w eurostar. com; from 2hrs 16mins) from London St Pancras to Gare du Nord in Paris. From Paris you can then pick up a train to Normandy with French rail provider **SNCF**, which runs a regional network, the TER (Transport Express Régionale; w sncf-connect.com/en-en/ter). There are fast, direct trains from Paris Saint-Lazare to Caen (2hrs 17mins), Bayeux (2hrs 18mins), Carentan (2hrs 43mins) and Cherbourg (3hrs 14mins). If you are coming from elsewhere in Europe, **Rail Europe** (w raileurope. com) provide routes between all major western European cities.

Very few towns and cities in Normandy are served by the train network so Caen, Bayeux, Carentan and Cherbourg are the only stations you are likely to use. You don't need to book in advance; just buy a ticket at the station. Timetable leaflets (*fixes horaires*) are available at all stations. Bikes are allowed on most trains, but check individual websites.

BY BUS All major coach companies go **from the UK** to Paris, including FlixBus (w flixbus.co.uk), BlaBlaCar Bus (w blablacar.co.uk/bus) and Megabus (w uk. megabus.com), taking from 9 hours 20 minutes. Then, you will have to find your way to Normandy; the train is quickest (see above), but if you prefer to take the bus from Paris to Caen, take FlixBus or BlaBlaCar Bus (from 2hrs 40mins).

Within Normandy, buses travel between the main cities and along the coastal roads, but most of them only run from once to four times a day, Monday to Saturday. **Nomad Car** (w nomad.normandie.fr) is the brand for all regional public transport in Normandy, including the bus companies operating in the region. Its website is only in French, but there are some useful maps (w nomad. normandie.fr/les-plans-du-reseau-nomad), and information for buses to and from a destination (w nomad.normandie.fr/itineraire). The price of a single bus

◀ 1 There are pretty towns aplenty in Normandy, but reminders of war are never far away, such as the remnants of Mulberry B Harbour at Arromanches-les-Bains (page 55). 2 British special forces storm Juno Beach at Saint-Aubin-sur-Mer (page 36) on 6 June 1944. 3 & 4 Visitors can pay their respects at memorials such as the impressive statue of US Navy sailors (page 89) in the dunes at Utah Beach and the vast British Normandy Memorial (page 48). 5 There are also informative and thought-provoking museums, including D-Day Experience near Carentan (page 85).

fare varies from €1.90 to €4.90 according to distance. You can pay on the bus with cash only. Otherwise, download the app Atoumod M-Ticket – although on the app you need to know the name of the transport network you are travelling on.

BY BIKE Many local tourist-information offices offer bikes to rent and have special World War II bike maps for sale. Cycling in Normandy is relatively easy on roads with cycle lanes, but there may be no cycle lanes on roads that lead to the smaller sites. Designated cycle routes all connect to a railway station; for more information visit w en.normandie-tourisme.fr/active-outdoor/cycling-in-normandy. The website includes an official D-Day landing beaches cycle route (VeloWestNormandy), but it only takes in certain landing beaches, then goes down to Mont Saint-Michel.

TOURIST INFORMATION AND TOUR OPERATORS

There are **tourist information offices** in towns and villages across Normandy, which are listed in the relevant chapters. Several useful websites cover a broader area: **Calvados Tourism** (w calvados-tourisme.co.uk) specialises in Calvados (to the southeast of Normandy, including Caen); **Manche Tourism** (w manche-tourism.com) covers the Manche *département* (including the Cotentin Peninsula); and **Normandy Tourism** (w en.normandie-tourisme.fr) covers the whole region. You can also find information at international tourist offices.

There is a huge range of D-Day landings and battlefield **tours**. We've listed some UK, US and local tour operators, while the International Guild of Battlefield Guides (w gbg-international.com) has around 300 professional guides who have undergone a tough accreditation. Its website has a search facility to find members who specialise in the locations or battlefields that most interest you.

INTERNATIONAL TOURIST OFFICES
Australia Level 22, 25 Bligh St, Sydney, NSW 200; +61 292 315 243
Belgium 222 Av Louise, 1050 Brussels; +32 25 05 28 10

Canada 1800 Av McGill Collège, Montréal, QC H3A 3J6; +1 514 288 2026
Germany Zeppelinallee 35–37, Frankfurt am Main 60325; +49 699 758 0148
The Netherlands Prinsengracht 670, 1017 KX Amsterdam; +31 205 353 010

South Africa Village Walk Office Tower Bldg, 3rd Fl, cnr Maud & Rivonia rds, Sandton; ✆+27 010 205 0201

UK The tourist office in London has now closed to the public, but try the websites w france.fr/en or atout-france.fr

USA 825 Third Av, New York, NY 1022; ✆+1 212 745 0967. Also 9454 Wilshire Bd, Suite 210, Beverley Hills, CA 90212; ✆+1 310 271 2693. Also 205 N Michigan Av, Suite 3700, Chicago, IL 60601; ✆+1 312 327 5200

BATTLEFIELD TOURS
UK tour operators

The Cultural Experience ✆UK 0345 475 1815; US toll-free +1 877 209 5620; w theculturalexperience.com. Scheduled small-group battlefield tours covering Operation Overlord.

Globus ✆0333 0165 644; w globusjourneys. co.uk. A mainstream tour operator with some D-Day tours.

In The Footsteps ✆01989 565599; w inthefootsteps.com. Small-group (6 people) 4-day tours from London in a minibus with a battlefield historian.

Leger Holidays ✆01709 385624; w legerbattlefields.co.uk. Longstanding battlefield tour specialists using well-known & respected guides. 4- to 5-day coach tours to Normandy.

Sophie's Great War Tours ✆07973 956373; w sophiesgreatwartours.com. Flexible tailor-made tours covering eg: D-Day preparations in the UK & the invasion in Normandy.

US tour operators

Band of Brothers Tours ✆+1 855 473 1999; w bandofbrotherstour.com. Based in Normandy & offering full-service battlefield tours to the US market, husband-&-wife team Severine & Ed Diaz worked together at the Utah Beach Landing Museum before setting up this tour company.

Collette Vacations ✆+1 800 340 5158; w gocollette.com. Operates a Memorials of World War II Tour that visits London, Normandy & Paris. Multiple departure dates each year.

EF Go Ahead Tours ✆+1 800 590 1161; w goaheadtours.com. Offers special-interest World War II tours that feature Normandy, other destinations in France and beyond.

Globus ✆+1 866 755 8581; w globusjourneys. com. US branch of this global company (see left).

Normandy American Heroes ✆+33 6 30 55 63 39; w www.normandyamericanheroes.com. Luxury, customised World War II tours all over Europe, but with a special focus on Normandy. Led by Rudy Passera, the only interpretive guide who has worked both for the Normandy American Cemetery and the Utah Beach Museum.

USEFUL APPS

There are three handy, free apps that provide extra information about events at particular locations:

D-DAY APP (w dday.app) This app has maps, photos, text and audio guides to 30 locations on the five D-Day beaches.

IN THEIR FOOTSTEPS (Dans Leurs Pas; w dansleurspas.com) Based on a set of seven yellow kiosks in Sword and Juno, which have photos, maps and summaries of what happened at each location, with the recollections of civilians and soldiers who experienced it. The app can be downloaded from QR codes on these kiosks.

REMEM'BERNIÈRES (w rememberniers.com) The seaside village of Bernières-sur-Mer has created two self-guided tours, 'They landed' and 'They freed our village', using information stands with historic photos and summaries of what went on. The app adds much more detail and can be downloaded from QR codes at each location.

Many **museums and tourist information offices** in France close for an hour or so at lunch. They are also sometimes closed completely on French public holidays.

Most **Commonwealth War Graves Commission** (CWGC) cemeteries are open 24/7; they do not charge an entrance fee.

Stephen Ambrose Historical Tours +1 888 903 3329; w stephenambrosetours.com. Founder Stephen Ambrose was a famous World War II historian. He literally 'wrote the book' – several, in fact, including *D-Day*, *Undaunted Courage* & *Band of Brothers*. He began leading tours in the 1970s & founded the D-Day Museum in New Orleans, which is now The National World War II Museum. His family continues with tours.

Local tour operators
Adrian Roads +33 6 58 13 73 35; w adrian-roads.com. Operating full- & half-day tours from Caen; also 2-day tours from Paris with overnight stop near Sainte-Mère-Église. Run by a Parisian & military-history enthusiast.
Allied Victory Tours +33 7 71 70 42 45; w alliedvictorytours.com. Private English or Dutch tours led by Mike van den Dobbelsteen, who takes part in reconstructions & is a collector of World War II memorabilia.
Bayeux Shuttle +33 6 07 19 54 05; w bayeuxshuttle.com. Run by an American, Adrienne O'Donoghue-Sion, who started visiting Normandy to see the graves of her relatives.
Blue Fox Travel +33 1 88 61 11 49; w bluefox.travel/paris/d-day-beaches-trip. Day tours to main Normandy beach sites from Paris, leaving at 07.00 & back by 20.00. Specific tours of the American & Canadian main sites.
Colin McGarry +33 6 10 89 56 71; w normandy-tour-guide.com. He has been guiding since 1982 & has a YouTube channel dedicated to D-Day history. Based in Bayeux.
D-Day 4 You +33 6 88 75 86 17; w dday4you. com. Local French guide, Magali Desquesne (fluent English-speaker) was born in Saint-Lô & now lives in Bayeux. She has been guiding in Normandy for over 11 years, has an encyclopaedic knowledge of World War II & is excellent at incorporating everyone (children included) in the tour. Her partner is Paul Woodadge (DDay Historian, see below).
D-Day Academy +33 2 31 08 47 88; w ddaca. com. Guided tours of key D-Day sites in World War II vintage vehicles.
D-Day Tours of Normandy +33 2 99 18 08 21; w d-daytoursnormandy.com. Run by a British couple who live in Brittany, this outfit offers 1- to 3-day tours of Normandy for individuals or groups of up to 4, or customised tours.
French Tours 01233 884 911; w french-tours. com. Chauffeured, guided private tours run by Michael Smith.
Gold Beach Company +33 9 67 82 05 14; w goldbeachcompany.com. Small local company of enthusiasts operating private or small-group full- & half-day tours in minibuses or jeeps.
Normandy Private Tours +33 2 77 15 22 30; w normandyprivatetours.com. Based in Caen, providing private chauffeur meeting you at Le Havre or Honfleur cruise terminals. Driver & audio guide only, though they can recommend tours aimed at American & Canadian beaches.
OverlordTour +33 7 89 00 28 41 (urgent calls only); w overlordtour.com. Based in Bayeux & offering full-day, half-day & 2-day tours, from Paris, Cherbourg & Ouistreham, or private bespoke tours. English-speaking French guides with minibus transport.
Paul Woodadge DDay Historian w ddayhistorian.com. Paul Woodadge is a well-known World War II historian & TV presenter, with a popular & influential YouTube history channel, *WW2 TV*. He also leads private bespoke tours. He is particularly strong on the less well-known sites. His partner is Magali Desquesne of D-Day 4 You (see left).
WW2 Veterans' Memories +33 6 76 24 14 84; w ww2veteransmemories.org. Small partnership offering half-day, 1-day & 2-day tours by minibus or jeep. They also work for the National D-Day Memorial in Virginia.

THE BIG SEVEN

For those short of time but self-driving or hiring a driver/guide, these are the 'Big Seven' key D-Day sites, running along the coast from east to west. Technically, you could do the whole trip in a day, but we wouldn't recommend it. You would have to severely limit how long you spend at each of the sites, and the non-stop driving time is 2½ hours (120km).

PEGASUS MEMORIAL MUSEUM This museum focuses on the dramatic taking of Pegasus Bridge at Bénouville by British glider forces (page 20).

JUNO BEACH CENTRE A museum that describes the Canadian Experience at Juno Beach (page 41).

D-DAY LANDING MUSEUM This explains how the Mulberry B artificial harbour, a colossal engineering masterpiece at Gold Beach, worked and what you can see of it now (page 58).

NORMANDY AMERICAN CEMETERY A vast site overlooking Omaha Beach (page 67).

POINTE DU HOC The dramatically crater-marked battery on this promontory was attacked by US Rangers after they bravely scaled the cliffs (page 75).

AIRBORNE MUSEUM Located in Sainte-Mère-Église, next to the church where parachutist John Steele was left dangling for two hours, this museum tells the story of US paratroopers in the early hours of D-Day (page 91).

UTAH BEACH LANDING MUSEUM Built right on the dunes and defences overlooking the beach itself, this has some fascinating and unique displays (page 88).

80TH ANNIVERSARY EVENTS IN 2024

A string of events were being planned at the time of writing to mark the 80th anniversary of D-Day. **Normandy Tourism** (w en.normandie-tourisme. fr/highlight/80th-anniversary-of-d-day) was organising many of the events, mainly in May and June 2024, including a show on 1 June using 2,500 drones lighting up the sky on the five landing beaches, plus a 30-minute sound and light show. Some events and exhibitions were set to take place in mid-October 2024. Separate commemorative events along the whole of the Normandy coast and inland were being planned by many of the museums and sites, both large and small.

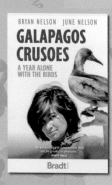
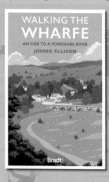
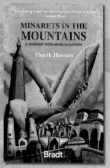

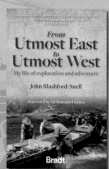

Part Two

THE NORMANDY COAST

3

Sword Beach and Around

Long sandy beaches stretch along the coast, where many small, modern holiday homes have panoramic windows looking out to sea. Today, the area designated as Sword Beach in the D-Day landings operation is full of families enjoying this resort area: walking their dogs, cycling along the promenade, swimming, picnicking or sand-yachting. It's difficult to imagine the bitter fighting that took place here on 6 June 1944, until you start exploring the many memorials, museums and other sites that bear witness to the assault.

Sword Beach, which was the easterly end of the D-Day landing beaches, runs for 9.5km, from Ouistreham in the east, at the mouth of the Orne River, to Luc-sur-Mer in the west.

Allocated to the British, it was perhaps the most critical of all to the success of Operation Overlord. The German 21st Panzer Division, a rapid defence force, was poised just southeast of Caen, ready to counter-attack any invasion force that attempted a landing along the coast. More immediately, the formidable 100mm guns of the Merville Gun Battery, built on a hillside to the east of the Orne estuary, were in position to defend Sword Beach and the Orne River.

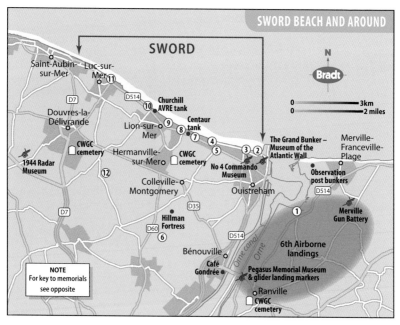

To appreciate fully the story of Sword Beach, start east of the beach itself, across the Orne River and canal. On D-Day, several hours before troops began landing on any of the beaches, around 8,500 men of the 6th Airborne Division were parachuted in or landed in gliders between the Orne and Dives rivers. The British 3rd Infantry Division landed on Sword Beach, supported by the 1st Special Service Brigade of commandos, led by Brigadier Lord Lovat (page 19).

The capture by the airborne troops of key bridges over the Orne River and the canal that runs parallel to it, both running 14km inland to Caen, had to be done at lightning speed. The plan was to hold off any counter-attack and take the prized objective, Caen, by 7 June – which was an overly ambitious schedule, as it turned out.

Caen wasn't captured until 19 July, 43 days after D-Day (page 126). But what the Allied airborne units did achieve on D-Day was vital: they captured the bridges and temporarily disabled the Merville Gun Battery.

GETTING THERE AND AROUND

Situated at the mouth of the Orne, Ouistreham is where the Portsmouth–Caen **Brittany Ferries** ships dock (page 5) and is the most direct route to the eastern end of the D-Day landing beaches from the UK. If you've taken your car on the ferry to Cherbourg, drive along the N13 to Ouistreham, bypassing Bayeux and Caen (136km; approx 1hr 40mins); see page 5 for how to reach the D-Day landing beaches if your ferry docks at Dieppe or Le Havre.

If **driving** around the region, the D514 coastal road from Ouistreham connects many of the coastal resorts and villages: travelling east, you reach Ranville (9.1km; 14mins), Sallenelles (12km; 17mins) and Merville-Franceville-Plage (15.1km; 20mins); and heading west, you pass through Hermanville-sur-Mer (2.3km; 5mins), Lion-sur-Mer (3.8km; 7mins) and Luc-sur-Mer (7.7km; 13mins). Douvres-la-Délivrande is a short drive inland from Ouistreham (9.8km; 15mins) or Luc-sur-Mer (4.1km; 9mins).

If you're coming to Sword Beach on public transport, you'll go to Caen (page 124) and travel on from there. Take the number 12 **bus** from Caen's Gare SNCF train station to Ouistreham (w twisto.fr/se-deplacer/itineraires/plans; 15.5km; approx 40mins). This route also continues to Colleville-Montgomery, Hermanville-sur-Mer and Lion-sur-Mer to the west. Nomad's 101 line (w nomad.normandie.fr/lignes-de-cars/ligne-101) runs from Caen to Douvres-la-Délivrande, Luc-sur-Mer and further west, to towns beside Juno Beach, while from June to September route 121 runs twice a day from Ouistreham to Bayeux via the coastal towns in this chapter.

Heading east, to get to Merville-Franceville-Plage, the Merville Gun Battery and the observation post bunkers, you will need a car or taxi. To get to Pegasus Bridge and Ranville, take the 12 bus from Ouistreham (1hr 10mins) or the 101 from Caen (48mins); then it's a short walk over the canal.

EAST OF THE ORNE RIVER

MERVILLE-FRANCEVILLE-PLAGE The seaside resort of Merville, as it's known today, which marked the eastern edge of the Normandy operation, was sidelined by the Allies. Their objective was the Merville Gun Battery, 2km south of the town, which remains the key site to visit today.

Merville-Franceville-Plage itself was liberated on 18 August 1944 by the Belgian Piron Brigade. A group of grey marble memorial stones in the centre of town commemorate the Belgian Piron Brigade, civilians and Allied soldiers killed in June, July and August, and the 35 men of 45 (Royal Marine) Commando who died in the opening skirmishes of 6–8 June 1944.

There's a **tourist information office** in the centre of town (1 av de Paris; ❜02 31 24 23 57; w normandie-cabourg-paysdauge-tourisme.fr; ⏱ Apr–Jun & Sep–Oct 10.00–13.00 & 14.00–18.00 Mon–Sat; Jul–Aug 10.00–13.00 & 14.00–18.00 daily; Nov–Mar 10.00–13.00 & 14.00–18.00 Tue–Sat).

What to see and do

Merville Gun Battery (Batterie de Merville, Pl du 9ème Bataillon; ❜02 31 91 47 53; w batterie-merville.com; ⏱ 15 Mar–30 Sep 09.30–20.30 daily, last entry 18.30; 1 Oct–15 Nov 10.00–18.30, last entry 17.00; adult/child €8/5) One of the best battery museums in Normandy, Merville Gun Battery stands on a hillside overlooking the Orne estuary and the beach at Ouistreham. Completed by May 1944, this easternmost defence was a vital part of Hitler's Atlantic Wall designed to stop an Allied invasion.

Well-preserved casemates (page 137), half buried under the grass, and underground bunkers are dotted around the 10ha windswept site. All four of the original 1.8m-thick, reinforced concrete gun casemates are open. Some bunkers were used for storing ammunition; others provided the kitchen and sleeping quarters. Films, themed exhibits inside the bunkers and boards placed everywhere around the site in French and English take you through the action.

Walk past a large hangar and a C47 (Dakota), which took part in the landings but has nothing to do with the original site, and head straight for one of the underground ammunition bunkers. A 20-minute drama-documentary, part-produced by the BBC, uses original footage to tell the story of the battery and the 9th Parachute Battalion (part of the 6th Airborne Division) who attacked under the command of Lieutenant Colonel Terence Otway. Otway's attack was dangerously compromised: he managed to gather just 150 of the 600 assigned troops at a crossroads approximately 1km from the battery. The other 450 men, along with the heavy equipment and weapons needed for the assault, had been dropped far from the rendezvous point. The 150 were armed with just Sten guns and grenades, one machine gun and small arms. At 02.50, in total darkness, they walked through minefields to the target, completely ignorant of what to expect.

In No 1 casemate, a sound-and-light experience (every 20mins) gives an idea of being in the thick of the fighting. At one end the German gun crew fires on the invasion fleet, while at the other, the casemate is attacked by Allied paratroopers. It may not be historically accurate, but it does give an idea of the conflict as the

---

1 The bunkers and gun casemates of Merville Battery were a key target for the Allies. 2 Café Gondrée in Bénouville was considered the first building to be liberated on D-Day. 3 The Pegasus Memorial Museum houses the original Pegasus Bridge. 4 & 5 British airborne troops used Horsa gliders – of which there is a full-scale replica at the Pegasus Memorial Museum. ▶

Second Lieutenant Raimund Steiner was acting commander of Merville Gun Battery on D-Day. Steiner had taken over from Captain Karl-Heinrich Wolter who on 19 May had left the battery to visit his mistress and died in a bombing raid. Steiner was asleep in his observation post bunker when, at 00.26, he got a frantic call from his sergeant major. A glider had landed on the battery and the Germans were engaged in close-quarter fighting. Steiner and his men re-took the battery and managed to get at least two guns operational again (though Steiner later claimed all the guns were repaired). The German forces held out, with Steiner directing fire on to Sword Beach from his bunker, until 17 August, when he and his men made an orderly retreat north. He was eventually captured on 6 September 1944 in Ypres.

ground shakes and the sounds of explosions and gunfire fill the air. In fact, Merville Gun Battery was attacked and overrun in the early hours of 6 June by Otway and his men *before* the invasion fleet turned up.

Several memorials are dotted around the site, including a bust of Otway, a memorial to the airborne forces and a white marble cross of sacrifice. A red oblong stone (/// shops.grasshopper.motion) marks the spot where Otway's group gathered for their attack.

Observation post bunkers (Within La Redoute bird sanctuary, chem de la Baie, 3km northwest of the museum; /// closure.organically.culminates; free) Visit Merville Gun Battery before these bunkers to understand the strategic importance of the observation post, which overlooks the Orne estuary and Sword Beach. The area is now a bird sanctuary, La Redoute, which takes its name from a small Napoleonic fortress the Germans occupied in June 1944 (150m east of the car park; closed to the public). The land is covered with gorse-like vegetation 2–3m high and criss-crossed by signposted footpaths; a circular path takes you past a fortified machine gun post, an anti-tank bunker and the observation post near the beach, used by the Merville Gun Battery commander, Raimund Steiner (see above). A small bunker 150m further east was originally designed to be the main observation post, but was actually used by Steiner to store his bicycle.

SALLENELLES Some 3km southwest of Merville, a grey memorial stone (beside the town hall car park at 29 rue André Pierre Marie) commemorates six Belgian and Luxembourg soldiers of the Piron Brigade, led by veteran commander Colonel Jean-Baptiste Piron, who lost their lives liberating Sallenelles on 14 August 1944.

RANVILLE AND BÉNOUVILLE The village of Ranville, situated around 8km southwest of Merville beside the Orne River, was the first to be liberated on D-Day by the British 13th Parachute Battalion, under the command of Lieutenant-Colonel Peter Luard. His ferocious response to the inevitable counter-attack resulted in 400 Germans being killed and 100 captured; he had ordered his men to hold fire until the Germans were within 50m. The 6th Airborne Division then set up their headquarters in Château du Heaume (2 rue du Colonel Fabien), now a private home which you can see from the gate. The capture of Pegasus Bridge across the Orne River, to the village of Bénouville on the west bank, was a crucial operation.

Today Ranville centres around the church and the CWGC cemetery. The nearest **tourist information office** is at Merville-Franceville-Plage (page 16).

What to see and do

CWGC cemetery (Rue de Comté Louis de Rohan Chabot; ⏱ 08.00–19.00 daily; free; ♿ after one small step at entrance) The cemetery was originally established in the churchyard of the Église Notre-Dame by the 591st Royal Engineers Parachute Squadron immediately after D-Day. Some of the early graves remain here, including the grave of the first Allied soldier killed in combat on the ground, Lieutenant Herbert Denham Brotheridge, who was shot leading his men across Pegasus Bridge (page 20) in the early hours of 6 June. The Gondrée family, whose café he was about to liberate (page 21), has placed a tribute plaque alongside his headstone. The main CWGC cemetery, the second largest British cemetery after Bayeux, contains 2,563 war dead, including over 300 German soldiers. The benches that every CWGC cemetery has are dedicated to the 8th Midland Counties Parachute Battalion and the 9th Parachute Battalion.

Inside the large church, light streams through the stained-glass window, which commemorates the 6th Airborne Division; small memorial plaques hang on the walls. Over the road a memorial park displays photographs of some of the soldiers

BRIGADIER LORD LOVAT

Simon Fraser, the 15th Lord Lovat, commander of the 1st Special Service Brigade of four commando regiments, landed on Sword Beach with his personal piper, Bill Millin (page 26).

A battle-hardened leader, Lovat had led successful raids earlier in the war, including on the Lofoten Islands in Norway in March 1941 and, with just 150 men, on the French coastal town of Hardelot. In August 1942 he commanded one of the only successful missions of the otherwise disastrous Dieppe Raid, winning the Distinguished Service Order. (The raid was designed to test Allied amphibious warfare tactics and equipment, gather intelligence and boost morale. But of the Allied forces, more than 3,600 were killed, wounded or captured; the Canadians suffered the worst, losing more than 68% of their troops.)

At 08.40 on D-Day, the Special Service Brigade landed on Sword Beach, at Colleville-Montgomery. After taking German posts in Ouistreham, Lord Lovat led his commandos inland to rendezvous with Major John Howard's paratroopers at Bénouville (Pegasus) Bridge (page 20). They arrived at the bridge only 2 minutes behind schedule, for which Lovat apologised, though some historians suggest it was more like an hour late. Let's not quibble; either way it was a remarkable achievement.

WIKIMEDIA COMMONS

Lord Lovat in 1942.

The other myth is that, as played by Peter Lawford in the movie *The Longest Day* (page 24), Lovat wore a white jumper on D-Day. He didn't – he wore normal battle dress. But why get in the way of a good dramatic scene?

who took part in the air drop, accompanied by short, poignant insights (in French and English) into their thoughts and actions that day. One, Alastair Mackie, was originally assigned to the same aircraft as his brother: 'I took my brother to one side, and kidded him that he should stay in my aircraft and enjoy the quality of service on offer; we agreed that, for family reasons, he must go with someone else.' They both survived. Don't miss the small plaque on the ground that remembers Major Jack Watson, who led the troops liberating Ranville. He was awarded the Military Cross, made a Chevalier de la Légion d'Honneur, and became an honorary citizen of Ranville before his death in 2011. The memorial plaque ends with: 'Jack, you will always remain in our memories.'

Pegasus Memorial Museum (Av du Major Howard; ☏02 31 78 19 44; w musee. memorial-pegasus.com; ⊕ 1 Feb–31 Mar 10.00–17.00 daily, 1 Apr–30 Sep 09.30–18.30 daily, 1 Oct–15 Dec 10.00–17.00 daily; adult/child €8.90/5.50) The museum, focusing on the operation to take Pegasus Bridge at Bénouville (see below), is located on an island a few metres from the current Bénouville bridge; this looks very similar to the original one, which was sold to the museum for 1 franc in 1994 and has pride of place in the grounds.

The museum explores the role of the 6th Airborne Division (British and Canadian troops) on the eastern flank, as well as the heroic and essential activities of the local French Resistance. Among the displays of equipment, arms and uniforms,

PEGASUS AND HORSA BRIDGES

The immediate and most critical action on 6 June was securing the bridges over the Orne River and its canal on the eastern flank of Sword Beach. A long thin island, running from Ouistreham to Caen 14km inland, separates the canal from the river to its east.

The first crossing point was at the village of Bénouville, 5km inland on the canal's west bank. A lifting bascule (counterweighted) road bridge crossed on to the island strip; 475m east, a second bridge spanned the river to the village of Ranville. After the events of 6 June 1944 these two bridges were known as Pegasus Bridge and Horsa Bridge respectively. The name 'Pegasus' came from the emblem worn by British airborne forces; 'Horsa' commemorated the British-built gliders that were used in Operation Overlord.

The 'coup de main' attack on the two bridges was given the codename Operation Deadstick: its purpose was to defend the whole eastern flank and stop the Germans attacking the D-Day landing beaches. In the west, American airborne forces would be doing the same, around Sainte-Mère-Église.

At 00.11 on 6 June, the first glider landed silently on the island at the east end of Pegasus Bridge, followed quickly by two others.

Two sentries on watch on each bridge and a garrison of 50 Germans were taken completely by surprise by the troops of the 2nd Battalion of the Oxfordshire and Buckinghamshire Light Infantry, led by Major John Howard (see opposite), and the paratroopers of the 7th Parachute Battalion. After a brief gun fight lasting just 10 minutes, Pegasus was taken, and Horsa soon after.

The Germans inevitably tried to counter-attack, but at 13.30 the surprising sound of the bagpipes of Bill Millin, Lord Lovat's personal piper (page 26), signalled the arrival of the 1st Special Service Brigade with their crucial supporting tanks.

A former soldier who had left the army to become a policeman in Oxford, John Howard was called up as a corporal in 1939. His rise was rapid: in 1942 he was promoted to major and given command of D Company, 2nd Battalion, Oxfordshire and Buckinghamshire Light Infantry. On D-Day he led them in the famous glider assault on Pegasus Bridge.

Major Howard was played by the actor Richard Todd in the movie *The Longest Day* (page 24), an entirely appropriate casting as Todd was actually there: he was a lieutenant in the 7th (Light Infantry) Parachute Battalion, 6th Airborne Division, dropped by parachute to reinforce the glider-borne troops on the bridge, which is where he met and fought alongside Howard.

look out for a set of bagpipes that belonged to Bill Millin (page 26), and photos and models of the extraordinary, huge Hamilcar gliders that carried heavy tanks. There's a 'Rupert' dummy paratrooper, which were small straw sacks roughly tied into a body shape and attached to a parachute as diversions (it looks nothing like the model featured in the movie *The Longest Day*; page 24). Well worth seeing is the documentary footage of D-Day and the work of the 6th Airborne shown on a loop in the circular cinema.

A full-scale replica of a Horsa glider (which you can walk through) brings home the huge risks taken by those flying in these silent, fragile aircraft, which frequently crash-landed in the trees. Made of plywood and canvas, they were remarkably vulnerable and the casualty rate of the men flying in them was devastatingly high. This one was constructed from the original plans and painted in the colours of the first Horsa that landed at Pegasus Bridge. Built by French and British aeronautical enthusiasts, it was unveiled on the 60th anniversary of D-Day in 2004.

The museum has some surprises, like the important role of the seemingly rather dull Bailey bridges, which get lost among the drama of glider landings and tank battles. Three of these huge sections of interlocking pieces of metal – looking like a Meccano set made for a giant – sit outside a hut where displays show their development. They were designed by one Donald Bailey to be assembled by 40 sappers in 2 to 3 hours. Capturing the bridges over the Orne River and canal was just the first step; expanding the beachhead and creating more crossings for the incoming Allied troops was an even greater challenge. In the ensuing weeks, the Royal Engineers built five Bailey bridges over the canal, 12 over the river, and another seven on the Dives River further east. 'I could never have maintained the speed and tempo of forward movement without large supplies of Bailey bridges,' Field Marshal Montgomery wrote in 1947.

Glider landing markers (On the riverbank south of the Pegasus Memorial Museum & D514) Take the path past the Liberty Tree, planted by the village of Bénouville in 2016 (note the moving inscription on the plaque), to the large white memorial stones marking where the three Horsa gliders touched down (see opposite). The first, carrying Major John Howard (see above), landed within 45m of the bridge. Up on the bank there's a mini 'signal monument' (page 138) put up in the 1950s; the German 50mm gun that guarded the bridge sits in a nearby gun pit.

Café Gondrée (12 av du Commandant Kieffer; ☏ 02 31 44 62 25; ⏱ 09.00–18.00 daily) At the west end of Pegasus Bridge, this family-run café was considered the first building to be liberated in France. Today it's a small room crowded with artefacts (many on sale) and a few old tables and chairs. Order the best cup of tea in Normandy and keep an eye open for the ducks who occasionally wander in hoping for snacks. The café is run by Madame Arlette Gondrée, who was a small child living at the café with her parents on 6 June. She especially welcomes ex-servicemen and their families (including the late Major Howard on various anniversaries), and is a key player in Normandy memorial events and anniversaries.

OUISTREHAM AND AROUND

Ouistreham, the coastal port city for Caen, is a pretty seaside resort where little wooden bathing huts line the Riva-Bella sandy beach and a lighthouse gives wonderful views over the surrounding countryside. On D-Day, Ouistreham marked the junction between the troops who landed on Sword Beach and the airborne troops who landed east of the Orne River and canal to secure the eastern flank. It has a good range of museums and smaller memorials to individual regiments and divisions.

TOURIST INFORMATION

Tourist office Esplanade Alexandre Lofi; +33 2 31 97 18 63; w caenlamer-tourisme.com; ⊕ Apr–Jun & Sep 10.00–13.00 & 14.00–17.00 daily; Jul–Aug 09.30–18.30 daily; Oct–Mar 10.00–12.30 & 14.30–17.00 Wed–Mon

Ouistreham Riva-Bella w ouistreham-rivabella.fr. This general website on Ouistreham and the area is run by the town hall.

WHAT TO SEE AND DO

The Grand Bunker – Museum of the Atlantic Wall (Le Grand Bunker – Musée du Mur de l'Atlantique, 6 av du 6 Juin; 02 31 97 28 69; w museegrandbunker. com; ⊕ Feb–Mar & Oct–mid-Nov 10.00–18.00 daily, Apr–Sep 09.00–19.00 daily, mid-Nov–16 Dec 10.00–18.00 Sat–Sun, 17 Dec–2 Jan 10.00–18.00 daily; adult/child €8.50/6.50) Le Grand Bunker stands on a residential side street, surrounded by small houses. Even in this incongruous setting, the 16m-tall bunker is impressive. It was a Hochleitstand, a German control tower and rangefinder for the artillery and anti-aircraft batteries covering the Orne estuary.

It was designed to be near-impregnable to a commando or even a full-scale infantry attack. Even if the assailants got through the heavily armoured door, they were faced with a 'killing zone' corridor, where they wouldn't be able to escape German fire, and more doors to get through before making their way up narrow spiral stairs to rooms on each level.

The bunker design was initially successful. On D-Day, French and British special forces failed in their initial assault and had to move on. Three days later, Lieutenant Bob Orrell of the Royal Engineers, with a team of three men, set two explosive charges against the door; it took 4 hours to finally break it open, but shocked by the successful attack, the German garrison of two officers and 50 men surrendered immediately. The liberation of Ouistreham was complete.

The five floors of the bunker have been restored to their June 1944 condition, complete with rather stiff but sufficiently lifelike models of German soldiers.

1 The impressive memorial to the Free French soldiers – known as La Flamme – in Ouistreham. 2 In Colleville-Montgomery there is a statue to Bill Millin, Lord Lovat's personal piper. 3 The interior of the Grand Bunker in Ouistreham has been restored to its 1944 condition. ▶

THE LONGEST DAY

The Longest Day film is inextricably linked to most people's understanding of what happened on 6 June 1944. Based on Cornelius Ryan's 1959 non-fiction book of the same name, the 3-hour black-and-white, star-studded movie is a drama-documentary telling the story of D-Day, hour-by-hour, beach-by-beach, soldier-by-soldier. The screenplay was written by Cornelius Ryan himself, and the producer, Darryl F Zanuck, hired a comprehensive team of advisers including veterans of D-Day. As a result, the movie, which premiered in France in 1962, is recognised as a remarkably accurate portrayal of the events of that longest of days.

The basement houses the generator room and ventilation room. Higher floors feature small, claustrophobic rooms which were the living quarters, infirmary, quartermaster's stores, control room, telephone switchboard and radio room. It's a relief to get up to the top floor, where the observation post's rangefinder is focused on Sword Beach.

D-Day 70th anniversary memorial (Esplanade Alexandre Lofi; /// wherein.logo.mallards) Situated right on the beach, the memorial features two angled stone pillars around a central plaque: the first lists the numbers involved on D-Day itself; the second lists those involved in the 70th anniversary, including 25 heads of state and 900 veterans of 4 Commando; and the plaque records Winston Churchill's words in 1948:

> Men will be proud to say: 'I am a European.' We hope to see a Europe where men of every country will think as much of being a European as belonging to their native land. We hope that wherever they go in the European continent they will truly feel: 'Here I am at home.'

No 4 Commando Museum (Musée no 4 Commando, pl Alfred Thomas; 02 31 96 63 10; w musee-4commando.fr; 8 Apr–12 Nov 10.00–13.00 & 14.00–18.30 daily; adult/child over 10/under-10s €5.50/3/free; ♿) Among the second wave of troops coming ashore on Sword Beach were the British 4 Commando unit, which was part of the 1st Special Service Brigade and led by Brigadier Lord Lovat (page 19), and the French commandos of Captain Philippe Kieffer (see opposite). They were tasked with knocking out a German strongpoint on the site of the old casino, as well as the guns along the beach. This private, one-roomed museum commemorating this event is crowded with artefacts, which the director will take you around if you ask. A model of Sword Beach in 1944 shows the headquarters of the Germans, originally the Hotel Saint George. The building is still there, next to the museum, now renamed the Hôtel Villa Andry. Among the many photographs is a famous black-and-white image of 4 Commando troops coming ashore in a landing craft; an annotated version beside it identifies the individuals, information that is rare to find. Some men wear steel helmets and some wear berets; the choice was left up to individual soldiers.

Memorial to the Free French soldiers (Bd Aristide Briand; /// towns.defeat.datable) Two short footpaths lead from the road up to this small but impressive memorial on a sand dune above the beach. A soaring metal sculpture shaped like a flame (it's popularly known as La Flamme), it stands on top of a sunken German blockhouse from the Atlantic Wall, topped with a French armoured turret from the Maginot Line (which had guarded the French–German border from the 1930s). Where they could, the Germans made use of captured materials, equipment and weapons; many of the guns used in the Atlantic Wall were former French and Czech guns that had been captured, and on their bunkers they used turrets from obsolete French tanks and bell turrets from the Maginot Line defences they had passed and defeated.

The memorial, which was unveiled on the 40th anniversary of D-Day, is flanked by two statues: of **Brigadier Lord Lovat** (page 19) and **Captain Philippe Kieffer** (see below), both of whom came ashore here. At their feet, ten small headstones carry the names of members of Kieffer's Commandos who were killed on D-Day in the attack.

FREE FRENCH HERO

Philippe Kieffer, hero of the Free French forces, was born in 1899 in Port-au-Prince, Haiti, where his parents had fled after Alsace was annexed by Germany in 1871. Before the war he had a distinguished career as a bank manager and director in Haiti, London and New York. The day before war broke out, he signed up with the French navy. He served on the battleship *Courbet* at Dunkirk and then, after the defeat of France, joined the Free French navy in Portsmouth on 1 July 1940.

Inspired by the British–Norwegian commando raid on the Lofoten Islands in March 1941, Kieffer persuaded his superiors to allow him to set up a commando unit, the Fusiliers-Marins ('Marine Riflemen'). The 20-man unit began training in harsh conditions at Achnacarry Castle in Scotland. Their first action was in August 1942 when 15 of his men distinguished themselves in the ill-fated Dieppe Raid: just over 6,000 Canadian and British troops were put ashore, and a few hours later over 3,600 were dead, wounded or captured; Kieffer's men covered the retreat of the troops. After this action, the existence of Free French Commandos was made public. During 1943–44 the unit grew in number and raiding experience. In April 1944 the unit became the 1st Battalion Fusiliers-Marins Commandos, aka 'Kieffer's Commandos', attached to No 4 Commando as part of Lord Lovat's 1st Special Service Brigade (page 19).

Kieffer and his 177 commandos were the only French soldiers to take part in the D-Day landings. Kieffer was wounded – first on landing, and then a second time while capturing the gun battery at the German casino strongpoint in Ouistreham – but he refused to be evacuated until 8 June. He returned five days later and continued to lead his men to Honfleur, Paris and beyond.

Tragically, as he was racing in a jeep to be one of the first to enter Paris – a moment of huge triumph for him and his men – his 18-year-old son, a member of the Resistance nearby, was killed by the Germans. Commandant Kieffer survived the war and went into politics. He also acted as military adviser to *The Longest Day* film (page 24) in 1962. He died later that year, the recipient of many awards including the French Légion d'Honneur, the Military Cross and an MBE, and is buried in the churchyard at Grandcamp-Maisy.

3

Around Ouistreham

Colleville-Montgomery Originally called Colleville-sur-Orne, this small commune just west of Ouistreham centre was renamed in June 1946 in honour of General Montgomery, commander of the Allied ground forces (see below).

Colleville-Montgomery is home to several monuments commemorating those who landed along this section of Sword Beach. Kieffer's Commandos **stone marker** (bd Maritime, at the junction with rue Vauban), a Modernist-style tableau of the landing of the French commandos, is very different from the usual memorials: carved into a large rectangular sandstone block, it shows figures in various poses, some lying on the ground, and the sea in the background. Around 100m west along the boulevard Maritime, a small **memorial stone** honours three of Kieffer's commandos who died here.

Further along the boulevard, at the place de Débarquement, is a **statue of piper Bill Millin**, one of the most well-known, and eccentric, characters of D-Day.

Millin, aged 21, was Lord Lovat's personal piper, who played 'Highland Laddie' as he came ashore under fire and as the brigade advanced inland to relieve airborne troops on the bridge at Bénouville (page 20). Pipers had been banned from the front lines after World War I as they had proved too much of a target. The story goes that Millin mentioned this when Lord Lovat asked him to take on the role. Lovat's reply was: 'Ah, but that's the English War Office. You and I are both Scottish, and that doesn't apply.' Millin's landing wasn't as dignified as the rest of his service on that day. He later told his son that when he jumped off the landing craft into a metre of water, his kilt floated up around him, making him look like a ballerina. Happily, his statue, erected in June 2013, remembers him looking every inch the hero he was.

A statue of **General Montgomery** (esp Montgomery, 2 rue des Rosiers) stands in its own small park set back from the beach. The 2m bronze statue by Vivien Mallock shows 'Monty' (see opposite) standing in his general's uniform.

Hillman Fortress (7 rue Suffolk Régiment, 3.7km inland; from the signposted parking area, walk into a field down a marked path; /// suggestions.unfocused. unbolted; ⊕ site daily; main bunker exhibits Jul–Aug 10.00–12.00 & 14.30–18.30 Mon & Wed–Sat; guided tours Jul–Sep 15.00 Tue; free) The Allies codenamed the German strongpoints in this sector after car brands – Morris, Daimler and Hillman. Called Hill 61 by the Germans, Hillman is a small, fortified site with 18 underground command bunkers. Hidden from view, these were the regimental headquarters of Colonel Ludwig Krug, commander of the German 736th Grenadier Regiment. From the top of this hill, 61m above sea level, he could see most of Sword Beach and direct his artillery and troops as needed. When the 1st Battalion Suffolk Regiment arrived, they discovered it hadn't been bombed or shelled as planned, but they attacked anyway. By the morning of 7 June, the Germans had had enough and surrendered. Some historians argue that this small delay was enough to scupper Montgomery's hope of reaching Caen on D-Day (page 126).

Hillman was a major site, but most of the bunkers remain hidden or closed. If you can, visit when the main bunkers, with their films and themed exhibits, are open. If not, QR codes on posts will trigger an audio description of what you're looking at, and information boards, placed around the site in French and English, explain the story.

Royal Norfolk Regiment memorial (Cnr of Les Longs Champs & rte de Colville, Biéville-Beuville) A dark-grey polished stone monument stands in memory of the 116 men of the Royal Norfolk Regiment killed between 6 June and 9 July 1944. The regiment had bypassed Hillman but suffered some casualties from the Germans garrisoned there. They lost more men when they continued up the hill to assist the 2nd Battalion Warwickshire Regiment, who were under attack.

HEADING WEST

HERMANVILLE-SUR-MER One of the popular seaside resorts along the coast, Hermanville-sur-Mer is just 2.6km from Ouistreham. Grand 19th- and early-20th-century villas line the road that runs along the beach. It was saved from major destruction when units from the British 3rd Infantry Division, who landed here on 6 June, quickly took it from the Germans that very morning, without prolonged fighting.

What to see and do

CWGC cemetery (Rue du Cimetière Anglais; &) This is one of the most tranquil military cemeteries in the area, reached down a quiet country lane and surrounded by woodland and fields of grazing horses. Very few people visit; the peace invites you to sit on a bench and contemplate the landings and the tragic loss of life. Some 900 identified servicemen are buried here along with 102 unidentified graves, most from the 3rd Infantry Division during the D-Day operation. Some of those killed in the Battle for Caen (page 126) in July 1944 and some from the fighting at the Falaise Pocket (page 117) in August 1944 have also been buried here.

Centaur tank (Cnr of rue Admiral Wietzel/D514 & rue du Dr Turgis) This British tank is not what it seems. A plaque calls it a Churchill AVRE (see below), and there *used* to be a Churchill AVRE tank on this spot, belonging to the Imperial War Museum, but it was returned to the museum in 2000 and replaced with this Centaur Dozer, a make which is normally turretless and has a bulldozer blade. The Centaur you see here is bladeless and has been retro-fitted with a Cavalier turret (same tank, different engine) and a 6-pounder gun. A new sign on the back now describes it as a Centaur Mark IV – which it almost is. Meanwhile the plaque remains unchanged because it's a memorial to *all* the 70 specialised tanks and their crews who landed on Sword and cleared the way for the following troops.

Beachside memorials You'll find a number of memorials within 250m of the Centaur tank, including the memorial to **sailors of the Allied Navies and Merchant Marine** (av Félix Faure, by the beach), a large stone commemorating the sailors of the Royal, Merchant and Allied navies who lost their lives in Normandy.

There is also a cluster around place du Cuirassé Courbet. Nearest the beach, the impressive memorial to **ORP *Dragon*** has a polished dark stone stele flanked on either side by a large, sculpted anchor. The Polish cruiser (ORP denotes 'Warship of the Polish Republic'), previously HMS *Dragon*, was stationed off Hermanville on 6 June 1944 and fired some 1,200 shells at onshore targets, successfully destroying a number of artillery pieces and six tanks, before returning to Portsmouth on 17 June to repair and re-arm. Back at her station off Sword Beach on 7 July, she was torpedoed in the early hours of the following morning. The engine room was hit, 37 Polish sailors were killed and 14 were wounded. Beyond repair, the *Dragon* was towed out and sunk to become part of an artificial reef off Courseulles-sur-Mer.

On the left of the ORP *Dragon* commemoration is the memorial to the **Norwegian sailors of D-Day**, a statue of a sailor carrying a shell, standing on a tall plinth.

AVRE TANKS

The most common type of Armoured Vehicle Royal Engineers (AVRE) was a Churchill tank, with a petard mortar replacing the normal gun. It was designed to blast bunkers by lobbing an 18kg high-explosive bomb, codenamed the 'Flying Dustbin', just over 70m.

Other versions of AVRE tanks were known as 'Hobart's Funnies', after Major-General Percy Hobart, who invented them with the kind of quirky genius displayed by 'Q' in the James Bond films. The tanks were equipped with flails for setting off mines, *fascines* (bundles of wooden sticks) for filling in trenches, torpedoes for blowing up barbed wire, and bridge sections for crossing trenches. They were pretty effective.

Inaugurated in June 2004 by King Harald V of Norway, it commemorates the 1,002-strong crews of the three Norwegian destroyers *Stord*, *Svenner* and *Glaisdale* (the first two torpedoed, the latter sunk by a mine), the three corvettes *Eglantine*, *Rose* and *Acanthus*, and the patrol boat *Nordkapp*.

The British **3rd Infantry Division** memorial, to the left of the Norwegian sailors, is a large black stone honouring the 'pioneers of the Allied forces' who landed at Hermanville-sur-Mer – they were the first to disembark on Sword Beach. The red triangle on a black background on the ground in front of the stone is the division's insignia. Around it are separate plaques dedicated to some of the division's units, including: the **2nd Battalion The Royal Lincolnshire Regiment** and the **2nd and 5th Battalions, East Yorkshire Regiment**, who landed in the first wave; the **13/18th Royal Hussars (Queen Mary's Own)**, a reconnaissance regiment; the **5th Battalion, King's Regiment (Liverpool)**, one of the oldest regiments in the British Army, dating back to 1685; the **five regiments of the Royal Artillery**, who were firing their guns from their landing craft as they approached the shore, and barely paused when they landed; and the **1st Battalion, South Lancashire Regiment (Prince of Wales's Volunteers)**, which lost 288 officers and men on D-Day and during subsequent campaigns. Along the west wall of the square, six boards display black-and-white historic photographs with text, in Norwegian and French, describing World War II from the Norwegian perspective.

LION-SUR-MER The pretty resort harks back to its 19th-century heyday, when substantial villas were built along the seafront for families who came for the healthy new pastime of sea bathing. But on 6 June 1944, Lion-sur-Mer was heavily defended by the German strongpoint (Allied codename 'Trout') at the western end of the commune. It had two auxiliary observation posts working for a battery at Colleville-Montgomery, a 75mm gun, two 50mm anti-tank guns and a heavy mortar gun. So, 41 (Royal Marine) Commando, part of 1st Special Service Brigade and tasked with taking the strongpoint and the German HQ (750m inland), wisely decided to land at Hermanville-sur-Mer and work their way through Lion-sur-Mer from the east. Most of the town was liberated on D-Day; the Trout strongpoint was taken the next day after the Germans withdrew overnight.

There's a **tourist information office** near the beach (rue Edmond Bellin; 02 61 53 60 02; w caenlamer-tourisme.com; Apr–Jun & Sep 10.30–12.30 & 14.30–18.00 Sat–Mon; Jul–Aug 10.30–12.30 & 14.00–18.30 daily).

What to see and do

Memorial to HM LCH 185 (On the promenade at the end of rue Marcotte) His Majesty's Landing Craft H 185 was a Royal Navy 'Headquarters' landing craft, whose role was to shepherd its group of landing craft across the Channel and on to the beach. It would then do the same for subsequent landings. On 25 June it was blown up and sunk by a naval mine. The memorial was unveiled in June 2018 by Telegraphist Patrick Thomas, a survivor of the sinking.

Churchill AVRE tank and 41 Commando sundial (Beside D514 at the roundabout with av de Blagny) The tank commemorates the landing of the 2nd Battalion, Royal Ulster Rifles and was unveiled on the 50th anniversary of D-Day by the battalion's commander, Sir Ian Harris. The battalion wasn't actually involved in the Battle for Lion-sur-Mer: they landed at noon and moved inland to Périers-sur-le-Dan.

The sundial and its plaque commemorate the liberation of Lion-sur-Mer by 41 Commando, who in fierce fighting saw 50% of their men killed, wounded or missing.

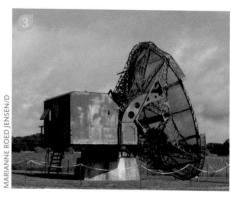

LUC-SUR-MER The small seaside village is terraced down to the beach where rows of colourful beach huts line the walkway along the sea. It was liberated on 6 June by **46 (Royal Marine) Commando**, as commemorated by a small square by the beach with a grey memorial stone (cnr of rue du Dr Charcot & rue du Général Dubail). Also within the square is a black stone dedicated to the **23rd Destroyer Flotilla** (British and Norwegian navies) which provided close-to-shore gun support at Sword Beach. It has a photograph of a destroyer, a list of the ships and the names of some of the men involved.

Like many of these resorts, it has its own **tourist information office** (45 rue de la Mer; 02 31 97 33 25; w coeurdenacretourisme.com; year-round 10.00–12.30 & 14.00–18.00 Mon–Sat).

DOUVRES-LA-DÉLIVRANDE AND AROUND

This small town, 3.5km inland, was just called Douvres during World War II. It was only in 1961 that the name was expanded to include the town's basilica, Notre-Dame de la Délivrande, which has long been a site of pilgrimage thanks to its black madonna. Douvres-la-Délivrande is well known for its basilica and for a nearby chapel with Lalique glass windows. But it also has some notable D-Day sites. Some **tourist information** is held at the Radar Museum (see below). The nearest tourist information office is in Luc-sur-Mer (see above).

WHAT TO SEE AND DO

1944 Radar Museum (Musée Station Radar 1944, rte de Bény; 07 57 48 77 32; w musee-radar.fr; Easter–Jun & Sep–mid-Nov 10.00–18.00 Tue–Sun, Jul–Aug 10.00–19.00 daily; adult/child €6.50/5; free guided tours; but the site is large, the ground is uneven & underground bunkers only have steps) The Germans' largest radar station in the Calvados region is a formidable site, even though the museum and its bunkers cover just a small part of the original station. A large German radar dish stands out on the windswept 10ha site on a high plateau outside the town. The underground bunkers have some excellent displays, artefacts and sophisticated models that explain the history of radar and the role of this radar station, and also a little of its impact on the local population. It's well worth taking a guided tour in English for small gems of information. Some local relations were considered so good that the commander allowed the postman to ride through the ultra-top-secret base on his bicycle to deliver letters to the village on the other side, thus saving him a 5km ride around the perimeter. What the postman saw provided vital information for the local Resistance. The large command bunker has been set out to show how the Luftwaffe servicemen and women lived and worked. Keep an eye open for the five strongrooms with steel doors on the lower level. Shortly after the base was captured by the Allies, the British Army Pay Corps moved in. Soldiers were paid in the currency of the country they were in, so for 2½ months these rooms were used to store thousands of French francs, Belgian francs, Dutch crowns, Danish krone and Deutsche marks.

CWGC cemetery (Rte de Caen/D7, south of the rue de la Fossette junction;) The sound of traffic on the nearby main road disturbs the peace of this cemetery,

◁ 1 A string of pretty resort towns, including Hermanville-sur-Mer, line the long stretch of Sword Beach. 2 The CWGC cemetery in Hermanville is one of the most tranquil. 3 The German radar dish in Douvres-la-Délivrande is visible from far away. 4 A Sherman tank comes ashore at Lion-sur-Mer on 7 June 1944.

but it doesn't detract from the feeling that is present in every CWGC cemetery – that of the tragic loss of so many young men. The cemetery contains 1,128 graves, including 944 Commonwealth servicemen (mostly British from Sword Beach and the advance on Caen), 65 unknown and 180 Germans. The graves mainly date from the landings on Sword Beach. Others were brought in later from the battlefields between the coast and Caen.

Polish Air Force memorial (3.5km from Douvres, in Plumetot village; D222, opposite the town hall) The impressive mirrored steel memorial has three Spitfire fighter planes that glint in the sunshine on steel strings stretched between the arms of the letter V for 'victory'. It was unveiled on the 75th D-Day anniversary and recognises the airmen of the Polish 131 (Fighter) Wing. Three squadrons, the 302 (City of Poznań), 308 (City of Kraków) and 317 (City of Wilno), flew from the nearby B-10 advanced landing ground (ALG; page 52) in Plumetot between August and September 1944.

Juno Beach and Around

Delightful small seaside holiday resorts run west along the Juno Beach coast, from the pretty seaside town of Saint-Aubin-sur-Mer through Bernières-sur-Mer to Courseulles-sur-Mer and Graye-sur-Mer. The 9km stretch is crowded in the summer months: the French come for a seaside holiday; foreign visitors, particularly Canadians, come to see the memorials, Canada House (page 38) and Juno Beach Centre (page 41).

Juno was not the original codename. The British and Commonwealth beaches were codenamed after fish – Swordfish, Goldfish and Jellyfish – and then shortened by dropping the 'fish'. Allegedly, Churchill considered 'Jelly' an inappropriate name for a beach on which a great many men might die, so it was changed it to 'Juno'.

Although Juno is generally recognised as the Canadian beach, it was not exclusively so. Along with the 14,000 Canadian troops that landed here, 8,000 specialist British units, including Engineers and AVRE tanks, accompanied them. Juno has offshore reefs that the landing craft needed to get over on the rising tide, so the landings here were the last of the five beaches. The first wave of Canadian troops were met with heavy fire from German machine guns and mortars. Many soldiers were killed or wounded as they struggled to advance across the open beach. Despite the heavy casualties, the Canadians gradually pushed inland, capturing key towns such as Courseulles-sur-Mer and Saint-Aubin-sur-Mer in the afternoon. By the end of the day, they had established a beachhead approximately 8km deep and 10km wide. The fighting on Juno Beach was one of the bloodiest battles of D-Day. The Canadians suffered more than 1,000 casualties, including over 350 dead, while the British suffered 243 casualties.

GETTING THERE AND AROUND

By **car**, the D514 coastal road from Ouistreham (page 22) continues past Saint-Aubin-sur-Mer (10.6km; 22mins), Bernières-sur-Mer (13km; 25mins) and Courseulles-sur-Mer and Graye-sur-Mer (16.6km; 32mins). Heading inland, Bény-sur-Mer is southeast of Courseulles (6.4km; 9mins). From Cherbourg, the N13 takes you through the Cotentin Peninsula sites, Colleville-sur-Mer and Bayeux to the Juno Beach Centre (126km; approx 1hr 34mins).

JUNO BEACH AND AROUND

◯ **Memorials**

1 North Shore Regiment (CAN) *p36*
2 Fort Garry Horse (CAN) *p36*
3 Bernières memorial, Queen's Own Rifles
   & others (CAN) *p38*
4 Inukshuk (CAN) *p39*
5 14th Regiment, Royal Artillery (CAN) *p39*
6 Courseulles liberation *p41*
7 Canadian & Scottish regiments
   (CAN, GB) *p41*
8 Royal Winnipeg Rifles (CAN) *p41*
9 1st Armoured Division (POL) *p42*
10 Juno Beach signal stone *p42*
11 Royal Winnipeg Rifles & Canadian
   Scottish Regiment (CAN) *p44*
12 Inns of Court Regiment (GB) *p44*
13 Bény-sur-Mer liberation *p45*
14 Fontaine-Henry liberation *p45*

By **train** from Cherbourg, take the regular TER to Bayeux (1hr 10mins) and then take the 121 bus. If you are travelling from elsewhere by train, alight at Caen and board the 101 bus. By **bus** from Caen, the 101 route takes in Saint Aubin-sur-Mer, Bernières-sur-Mer, Courseulles-sur-Mer and Graye-sur-Mer. From Ouistreham, take the 12EX into Caen, then the 101. From Bayeux, take the 121 via Bény-sur-Mer and Graye-sur-Mer to Courseulles-sur-Mer. From July to September, the 121 continues on to Ouistreham and back, via the main landing beaches, twice a day. For route details, visit w nomad.normandie.fr/lignes-de-cars.

Getting around is easy by **bicycle** as most places are on the D514 coast road. Each town also offers good **walking** routes.

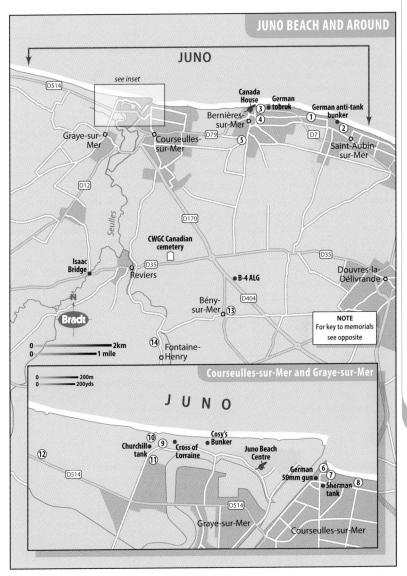

Saint-Aubin-sur-Mer is a pretty seaside town and, like many, owes its original 19th-century popularity to the fashionable new sport of sea bathing. Substantial Normandy villas, most of them rebuilt after the war, run along the seafront, while smaller houses line the streets behind. It marks the eastern end of Juno Beach and was the scene of fierce fighting, especially around the German strongpoint at the west end of the promenade.

This part of Juno Beach was targeted by Canada's North Shore (New Brunswick) Infantry Regiment and the amphibious tanks of its Fort Garry Horse (10th Armoured) Regiment, along with the British 48 (Royal Marine) Commando. Fighting was hard: many Canadians were killed in their landing craft by mines on the approach to the beach, and many on the exposed beach itself. However, when 48 Commando arrived 45 minutes later, the Canadians had cleared the way and the British commandos were able to pass quickly through the town.

There's a **tourist information office** by the beach (Digue Favreau; \ 02 31 97 30 41; w coeurdenacretourisme.com; ⊕ year-round; hours & days vary; check website), close to some of the memorials.

WHAT TO SEE AND DO At the west end of Saint Aubin's beach, tall poles flying the flags of nine Allied nations stand behind the **North Shore Regiment memorial** (by the junction of rue Canet & rue de Verdun). A central stone commemorates the capture of this beach by the Canadian North Shore (New Brunswick) Regiment, 'paving the way for 48 (Royal Marine) Commando'. Behind it, two smooth marble stones, shaped like open books, list the dead, one those from the Canadian units, the other those from 48 Commando and the civilians caught up in the fighting.

Just east of the memorial, by the sea wall, a formidable **German anti-tank bunker** protrudes on to the sand. It was particularly effective: its design meant the 50mm gun could fire along the beach, so once ashore, Allied troops and tanks came under a relentless barrage, which destroyed tanks and vehicles in the first waves of the landing. Meanwhile the gun crew inside was protected from offshore naval gunfire by thick reinforced concrete. The bunker was the centrepiece of the German 'resistance nest' at Saint-Aubin, surrounded by trenches, mines, barbed wire, machine guns and mortars. Along the beach, there were more machine gun and mortar positions, plus snipers firing from upstairs windows of the seafront villas. The bunker and its gun are surprisingly intact given that it was finally silenced by an AVRE tank, firing an 18kg high-explosive mortar bomb at it.

A further 100m east is the **Fort Garry Horse Regiment** memorial (rue Pasteur, northwest of the tourist information office), a plaque on a grey-brick slab commemorating the landing of the unit's tanks on D-Day.

BERNIÈRES-SUR-MER

Bernières-sur-Mer has a special place in Canadian hearts due to the mansion that is now called Canada House. While most of the town was destroyed, Canada House remained standing, occupying a prime position right on the beach. Bernières-sur-Mer was one of the five Canadian landing sites, involving the 8th Canadian

---

1 Canada House is one of the few buildings left from 1944 in Bernières-sur-Mer. 2 The German anti-tank bunker and its 50mm gun in Saint-Aubin-sur-Mer are surprisingly still intact. 3 The Bernières memorial was the first of the nine original signal monuments to be built. ▶

Infantry (Assault) Brigade, the Queen's Own Rifles of Canada, the Fort Garry Horse (10th Armoured) Regiment, and the guns of the 14th Field Regiment of Canadian Artillery (RCA). Although the fighting was hard at Bernières-sur-Mer, successive waves of Canadian troops pushed through the defences and the whole town was taken by the end of the morning.

The nearest **tourist information offices** are at Saint-Aubin-sur-Mer (2.5km) or Courseulles-sur-Mer (2.8km), or visit the informative **Remem'Bernières** website and app (w remembernieres.com; page 9).

WHAT TO SEE AND DO

Canada House (La Maison des Canadiens, 34 prom des Français; e maisondescanadiens@hotmail.fr; w maisondescanadiens.fr; free, but book in advance) One of very few buildings left from 1944, Canada House stands prominently on the promenade a few metres away from the signal monument (page 138). It had been requisitioned by the Germans, and Allied bombers deliberately left the house standing so it could act as a landmark for the Canadian troops landing on the beach on D-Day. Many of them sheltered on the beach behind the wall of Canada House. At 08.15, the Queen's Own Rifles entered the house, taking several German soldiers prisoner. It was the first house on Juno to be liberated on D-Day; photographs of soldiers with local French citizens appeared in Canadian newspapers, and the house became an icon to those at home.

Nicole Hoffer, the welcoming and enthusiastic owner of the handsome three-storey villa, which was bought by her grandparents Edmond and Cécile Hoffer in 1936, shows visitors photographs and objects that fill the main living room. Many of these have been given to her over the years by veterans, and each one has an intriguing story. A small cross was picked up by a Canadian soldier, who put it in his top pocket; he was hit in the chest but was not injured, while the cross lost an arm. Then there's the life-saving story of the two 100-franc notes handed over by… We won't spoil it for you. Along the west wall of the house, a series of black-and-white contemporary photographs and text tell the story of the Canadian landings here.

Every year on 6 June, Nicole Hoffer, friends and locals, visitors and Canadians, gather on the beach. As the sun goes down, they light small lanterns and launch them into the sea in a moving and unforgettable remembrance of the fighting.

Memorials The **Bernières memorial** (pl du 6 Juin), a large concrete slab right in the centre of the square, was the first of the original nine 'signal' monuments (page 138) to be built. The first stone was laid at a ceremony on 6 June 1949, attended by Field Marshal Montgomery (page 26). Somewhere buried inside is a copper shell casing with the text of his speech made that day.

A German anti-tank bunker (prom des Français, 180m east of Canada House on the seafront) no longer has its gun, but is covered with plaques to units including: the 800 men of the **Queen's Own Rifles of Canada**, who came ashore on this spot and of whom 143 were killed or wounded; the Canadian **Stormont, Dundas and Glengarry Highlanders**, aka 'The Glens', who also stormed this beach; and the British **5th (Hackney) Battalion, Royal Berkshire Regiment**, who stayed on to defend the beach. Next to the bunker is a commemorative stone to the Canadian **Fort Garry Horse Regiment**, who supported them, and another to **Le Régiment de la Chaudière** (Québécoise). The name 'la Chaudière' puzzled the French – they translated it literally as the 'Regiment of the water boiler', but it was actually named after Canada's River Chaudière. The last stone, in the form of a lectern, was placed in 1999 by the Historic Sites and Monuments Board of Canada. It has a metal contoured map showing where the Canadian forces landed and where they went from Juno.

Canada's Inuit soldiers are honoured at the **inukshuk memorial** (rue Victor Tesnière, set back a little from the road; /// courts.domino.ruby), a stack of rough-hewn stones. The word 'inukshuk' means 'in the likeness of a human' and the stones are placed as if a child had drawn a figure with arms outstretched. Stone markers such as this, made for centuries by the Inuit, can be way-markers, warning signs or just marks to highlight places of honour. This inukshuk was created by Bernières local Pierre Leberon on the 60th anniversary of D-Day (2004), dedicated to Canada's First Nations soldiers. Another stands outside the Juno Beach Centre in Courseulles-sur-Mer (page 41).

Heading inland by 1km, a reddish stone memorial lists ten men of **C Company, 14th Field Regiment, Royal Canadian Artillery** (cnr of rte de Bény & chem dit de Reviers). They died on D-Day in the field behind, when four of their M7 Priest self-propelled gun vehicles were ambushed by a German 88mm gun firing from a bunker concealed in the trees of the Bois de Tombette, 2.5km away. The memorial was an initiative of the commander of the troop, Lieutenant Garth Webb, who also founded the Juno Beach Centre in Courseulles-sur-Mer (page 41). It was installed in 2006.

German tobruk (Prom des Français, 100m east of the memorials) The sealed-up concrete tobruk (page 138) has information boards with **Remem'Bernières** QR codes (page 9) about the bunker and a 19th-century house behind the sea wall. It was briefly used as a German HQ before being demolished to make way for fortifications.

COURSEULLES-SUR-MER AND GRAYE-SUR-MER

The pretty fishing port of Courseulles-sur-Mer is a popular seaside resort, with a marina, a daily fish market, small streets bustling with shops and cafés, and bars and restaurants that look out over the sea. It is tranquil now, but on D-Day, 14,000 Canadians in two brigades of the Canadian 3rd Division landed between Courseulles-sur-Mer and Saint-Aubin-sur-Mer. At Courseulles-sur-Mer itself, fighting was fierce on both banks of the Seulles River. On the west side, the beach was protected by sand dunes, which the Germans had fortified with bunkers, barbed wire and mines. The bunkers had to be painstakingly taken one by one, but by the afternoon the town was in Canadian hands. Today, the Seulles River splits Courseulles-sur-Mer on its east bank from the commune of Graye-sur-Mer on the west bank – aside from a small sandy spit on the west side which belongs to Courseulles and is the site of the Juno Beach Centre (page 41). There's a **tourist information office** (5 rue du 11 Novembre, Courseulles-sur-Mer, east bank; ☏ 02 31 37 46 80; w coeurdenacretourisme.com; ⊕ year-round 10.00–12.30 & 14.30–17.00 Mon–Sat).

WHAT TO SEE AND DO
The east bank
Sherman tank (Quai des Alliés; opposite the children's carousel by the mouth of the Seulles River) The tank is adorned with the badges of the military units that landed on this section of Juno Beach. They were a part of the 7th Canadian Infantry Brigade, supported by the 6th Canadian Armoured Regiment (the 1st

OLRAT/D

BOUTTIME/D

RODFERRIS/D

PACK-SHOT/S

Hussars), who dedicated this tank to the memory of those who died on this section of the beach.

This amphibious version of the Sherman tank is called a 'DD' (Duplex Drive, with both tracks for land and propellers for water). You can see the transmission gears at the back, which drove the two propellers, but the propellers themselves are missing. The metal boat-shaped frame around the base of the canvas skirt kept the tank afloat. These frames were usually cut away with the skirt when the tank was safely ashore – except this one never made it to shore: It sank and was recovered 27 years later.

German 50mm gun (Quai des Alliés) Standing rather incongruously next to the carousel, the gun was in a bunker closer to the beach, and originally part of the Widerstandsnest defences at the mouth of the Seulles River. Jagged shell holes in the gun shield show its vulnerability against heavy weaponry.

Memorials A large stone **liberation monument** (pl Charles de Gaulle), surrounded by flags, honours the Allies who freed Europe, and General Charles de Gaulle, 'the liberator', who came ashore by Courseulles on 14 June 1944 on a quick visit to newly liberated France (page 63).

Further east, two plaques on small stone blocks, to **Canadian and Scottish regiments** who landed here, stand either side of some steps down to the beach (opposite the car park off av de la Combattante; /// galleries.lawgiver.embarrassed). They remember the 458 officers and men of the Regina Rifles who fell on D-Day; the British Royal Engineers 961 and 966 Inland Water Transport companies, who landed with the Canadians and operated ferries getting supplies ashore; the Canadian Scottish Regiment; the Belgian Volunteers (the Piron Brigade); and the 3,504 men from the 8th Battalion, Royal Scots, 6th Battalion, Royal Scots Fusiliers and 6th Battalion, King's Own Scottish Borderers, who landed on Juno on 13–14 June, and subsequently gave their lives liberating Europe.

The **Royal Winnipeg Rifles** memorial (120m east along the seafront promenade, at the junction with rue Pierre Villey) is unusual in that it is made of wood. Erected on the 20th anniversary of D-Day (1964) and marking the point at which the regiment came ashore, it features a teak crusader's sword, embedded point down in a plinth of Manitoba granite, which is a reference to the 'Great Crusade' that General Eisenhower mentioned in his printed Order of the Day, sent to the 175,000 troops of the expeditionary force on 5 June 1944 (page 82). The base features the regiment's emblem: a rampant devil with a torch, based on their nickname 'Little Black Devils', after the dark tunics they wore in 1885. There is another memorial to this regiment in Graye-sur-Mer (page 44).

The west bank

Juno Beach Centre (Voie des Français Libres; 02 31 37 32 17; w junobeach.org; Feb–Dec daily, hours vary, check website; adult/under-8 museum only €7.50/free, museum & bunker €12/free;) Juno Beach Centre is right at the edge of the shoreline by the mouth of the Seulles River. The large modern building, with a curved metal roof that catches the sunlight, is more of an interpretation journey

4

◁ 1 The 18m-tall Cross of Lorraine stands high on the dunes. 2 Outside the Juno Beach Centre in Courseulles-sur-Mer, an inukshuk cairn honours Canadian indigenous soldiers. 3 The Canadian cemetery in Bény-sur-Mer bears witness to the country's sacrifice on Juno. 4 Juno Beach Centre's memorial kiosks record the names of Canadians who served in the two world wars.

than a traditional museum, telling an intriguing story that non-Canadians know little about. It explores how and why a million Canadians fought a war they weren't obliged to fight, who those men were and what their experiences were like. One of those who came ashore on 6 June 1944 was Garth Webb, a lieutenant in the Royal Regiment of Canadian Artillery. He returned 50 years later and, noting the lack of a centre to mark the role Canadians played on D-Day, he started fundraising; Juno Beach Centre opened in 2003.

Galleries explain the pre-war Canadian psyche and political background, mobilisation and training, and the campaigns fought by the Canadians in both world wars. Particularly moving are video testimonies from soldiers and the drawers of personal effects of soldiers who never returned home.

Outside are a range of monuments and statues. There's a set of **memorial kiosks,** inverted cone-shaped pillars covered with commemorative 'bricks' (metal plaques). Each one has been purchased by donors who want to record the names and details of Canadians who served in the two world wars, as well as those who were in the military in peacetime or in other conflicts around the world. Two statues stand out: the striking, modern **Remembrance and Renewal** sculpture by Colin Gibson features five cloaked soldiers melded together; while an **inukshuk cairn** honours Canada's 'First Nations, Métis and Inuit soldiers who served in Europe during the Second World War'.

There's also a rectangular stone commemorating the **sailors of the Royal Canadian Navy** who were lost during World War II. In front of it, a series of granite pillars tell more of the story.

Various pieces of military hardware and anti-tank obstacles stand on the scrubland between the centre and the sea. There are guided tours into a **German observation post** which co-ordinated fire from local batteries, and a **German command post bunker**, only uncovered in 2010, that was used by Hauptmann Grote, commander of 6th Company, 736th Infantry Regiment. He had a window cut into the wall to let light in, which rather defeated the point of a bunker in the first place!

Cosy's Bunker (300m west along the shore from Juno Beach Centre; /// convenes. ebbed.blurts)

The task of knocking out this German pillbox was assigned to Lieutenant W F 'Cosy' Aitken and his squad of 15 men from B Company, Royal Winnipeg Rifles. After a tough fight, they took the bunker and handed the task of blowing it up to the Royal Canadian Engineers, who did a pretty good job, hence the dramatic tilt of the heavily damaged bunker into the sand. Cosy was wounded in the chest but recovered and was back with his company within three and a half months.

Cross of Lorraine (Off voie des Français Libres, Graye-sur-Mer; northwest of the car park; /// illustration.seminal.plush)

Standing up on the dunes, the 18m-tall stainless steel cross, which was inaugurated on the 20th anniversary of D-Day (1964), can be seen from afar. It's located 128 metres east from where General de Gaulle came ashore on 14 June (see opposite) and has his name at its base.

Fifty metres southwest, on the roadside (/// dictionary.fussily.notated), a black polished stone with the coat of arms of Poland commemorates, in French and Polish, the **Polish 1st Armoured Division**, which was attached to the Canadian 1st Army and came ashore here in late July 1944. Along the footpath, 140m west (/// headliner.nosed.electrodes), the official mini **signal stone** for Juno Beach is inscribed with a rather bland statement underplaying the significance of this spot: 'Here on 6 June 1944 Europe was liberated by the heroism of the Allied Forces.'

A string of important figures landed at Graye-sur-Mer, which had been designated as a post-D-Day landing zone. On 7 June, **General Bernard Montgomery** (page 26), commander of all Allied ground forces for the Normandy operation, disembarked from HMS *Hilary*, moored just off the beach, on to a Canadian amphibious truck, which delivered him and his aide-de-camp ashore. There is famous black-and-white newsreel footage of him jumping down from the truck on to the beach. He was then driven off in a jeep through the dunes and away to his mobile headquarters, 9km inland in the grounds of Château de Creullet at Creully (page 53).

Prime Minister **Winston Churchill** was the next VIP to land here. He had intended to be present at the landings on 6 June, but was eventually persuaded by King George VI to wait until the beachheads were secured. Champing at the bit, Churchill crossed the Channel on 12 June, despite a warning from Montgomery that German snipers were still about. With Churchill were the head of the British Army, Field Marshal Sir Alan Brooke, and Jan Smuts, who was the South African prime minister and a British Army field marshal. Montgomery met them on the beach and took them to his headquarters (page 53) for lunch.

Two days later, on 14 June, **General Charles de Gaulle** (page 63), leader of the Free France government-in-exile, crossed the Channel on the destroyer *La Combattante* and was transferred by landing craft to this spot at around 13.30 (as marked at the Cross of Lorraine, see opposite). He went on to greet General Montgomery at his HQ before heading to Bayeux to declare it the first Free French city (page 63). He then visited Isigny-sur-Mer and Grandcamp-Maisy in the Omaha Beach sector before boarding *La Combattante*, which had been waiting off Courseulles, at sunset.

On 16 June, **King George VI** turned up on this beach and was whisked off to Montgomery's HQ.

Churchill en route to Juno Beach on 12 June.

GEOPIX/A

Churchill tank (voie des Français Libres, Graye-sur-Mer; northeast of the junction with av du Général de Gaulle; /// reserves.swindles.composites) In the early morning light of 6 June, British troops from 26 Squadron, Royal Engineers drove this tank, a 290mm spigot mortar variant of the AVRE tank (page 28), off its landing craft just near here, and straight into a 4m-deep bomb crater concealed by flooding behind the dunes, where it became hopelessly stuck. Four of its six-man crew were shot and killed trying to escape. The tank was left in place and used by the Allies as a foundation for a temporary bridge over the flooded area. In 1976, British Army Engineers pulled it out of the ground and restored it to its current condition. One of the two surviving crew, driver Bill Dunn, died in 2014 and, in accordance with his last wishes, his ashes were scattered next to his tank.

Other memorials A rough-hewn stone near the Churchill tank (on the edge of the car park off av du Général de Gaulle, Graye-sur-Mer; /// confines.autographs. blog) commemorates the **Royal Winnipeg Rifles** and the **Canadian Scottish Regiment**, who suffered heavy casualties capturing the village of Graye-sur-Mer. Another memorial marking the landing point of the Royal Winnipeg Rifles is 1.5km away in Courseulles-sur-Mer (page 41), which shows how much of Juno Beach they covered.

Further inland, a large pink marble block commemorates one of the less well-known assaults on D-Day by the British **Inns of Court Regiment** (650m east on D514, in a field next to the road; /// wobbly.preservation.circus). The regiment, which dated back to the 16th century, was given the nickname 'The Devil's Own' in the 18th century by King George III when he learnt that the unit was composed of lawyers. On D-Day, C Squadron of the light tank regiment were attached to the 3rd Canadian Infantry Division, landing in this area 30 minutes after the first wave. Their almost-impossible job was to race ahead in their armoured scout cars up to 50km behind enemy lines to blow up the main crossings along the Orne River south of Caen. Despite a heroic attempt, their small units were whittled down, by Allied friendly fire (page 131) as well as German shells, and they were unable to reach their primary objectives.

BÉNY-SUR-MER AND AROUND

The small village of Bény-sur-Mer is located not by the sea but 13km inland, south of Bernières-sur-Mer. Its château and church, largely reconstructed in the 19th century, survived the fighting. It was a German artillery command post, which was captured on D-Day by Le Régiment de la Chaudière, supported by the tanks of the Fort Garry Horse Regiment. The nearest **tourist information office** is at Luc-sur-Mer (page 31).

WHAT TO SEE AND DO
CWGC Canadian cemetery (D35, 1km east of Reviers; signposted from D404 & Reviers; parking on Les Ruraux road) This cemetery, situated on a minor road surrounded by farmland, with tractors and few cars driving past, occupies a large space stretching out from an extensive green lawn. Two stone towers frame the entrance, one facing towards the sea, the view obscured over the years by trees, the other overlooking the cemetery itself, which contains the graves of 2,025 known and 19 unknown Canadians, plus four British soldiers and airmen. Among them are those of three brothers from Toronto. George Westlake, serving with the North Nova Scotia Highlanders, died on 7 June, while Albert and Thomas, serving with

the Queen's Own Rifles, died together four days later on the advance towards Caen. Albert and Thomas Westlake are buried together as they were found, while George is in another section.

Isaac Bridge (D176, 900m west of Reviers, crossing the Seulles River) Blink and you might miss this as you drive past, especially since there's little left of the amazing do-it-yourself bridge built by 183rd Field Company of the British Royal Engineers. Back then there was an old, narrow, three-arch masonry bridge over the river here, but it was causing a bottleneck. On 14 June, the Royal Engineers, who had neither bridging materials nor their vehicles, which had been held up, were ordered to build a second bridge to alleviate the traffic jams. They had to improvise and find the materials they needed locally. They made use of an existing stone plinth on the west bank (still there) a few metres downstream, to support one end. They also built two support piers mid-stream using six ingeniously scrounged, discarded 'Roly-Polys', 1.2m-wide drums which were wrapped with steel matting and attached to the front of AVRE tanks, to roll out this matting over soft areas of ground. The engineers worked at a furious pace and by the end of 20 June, the new bridge, named after the company commander Major Isaac, and its approach roads were finished. There is a memorial stone on the east bank.

Memorials The **Liberation of Bény-sur-Mer monument** (D79, next to the Salle des Fêtes in the middle of the village), a metal plaque on a small stone, commemorates the liberation on D-Day by Le Régiment de la Chaudière.

In the nearby village of Fontaine-Henry, another **liberation monument** (D170, by the bus stop) is easy to miss. Tucked into a small space in front of a garden railing, the small marble tablet simply lists the Canadian liberators of the village in the evening of D-Day: the 6th Canadian Armoured Regiment (the 1st Hussars), Le Régiment de la Chaudière, the Regina Rifles, 13th RCA Regiment, Royal Canadian Horse Artillery and the Royal Canadian Electrical and Mechanical Engineers. It was principally B Company of the Regina Rifles who liberated Fontaine-Henry, losing 11 men in the process, but the others passed through, so they are all mentioned. The monument was erected on the 50th anniversary of D-Day (1994).

At the **B-4 advanced landing ground** (ALG, page 52; park in the lay-by on the northbound side of D404 & climb up the bank; /// symmetries.arctic.difficult) A small stone plaque commemorates the Royal Canadian Air Force squadrons 401, 411 and 412, who were based at this ALG between 18 June and 7 August. Like many such memorials there are photos or small personal plaques placed here by relatives.

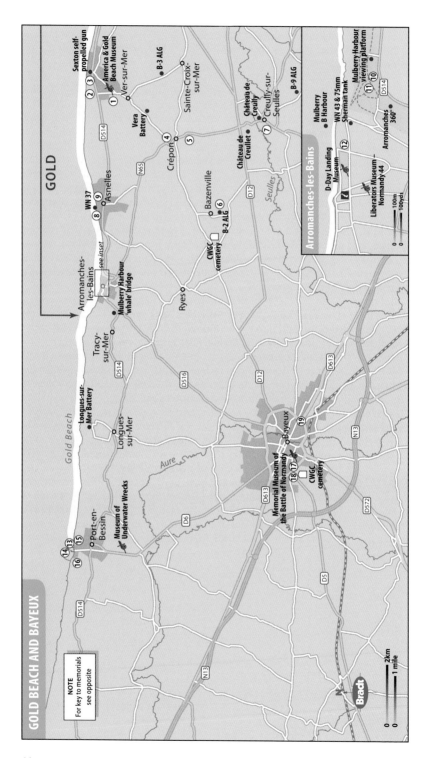

GOLD BEACH AND BAYEUX

NOTE
For key to memorials
see opposite

GOLD

Gold Beach

Arromanches-les-Bains

Sexton self-
propelled gun

America & Gold
Beach Museum

Ver-sur-Mer

B-3 ALG

Sainte-Croix-
sur-Mer

B-9 ALG

Château de
Creully

Creully-sur-
Seulles

Vera
Battery

Crépon

Château de
Creullet

Seulles

Bazenville

B-2 ALG

Asnelles

WN 37

CWGC
cemetery

Mulberry Harbour
'whale' bridge

Ryes

Tracy-
sur-Mer

Longues-sur-
Mer Battery

Longues-
sur-Mer

Aure

B-9yeux

Memorial Museum of
the Battle of Normandy

CWGC
cemetery

Port-en-
Bessin

Museum of
Underwater Wrecks

Arromanches-les-Bains

Mulberry
B Harbour

Mulberry Harbour
viewing platform

WN 43 & 75mm
Sherman tank

Arromanches
360°

D-Day Landing
Museum

Liberators Museum –
Normandy 44

see inset

5

Gold Beach and Bayeux

Large flat fields of arable crops, separating small villages, run down to a gentle curve of sandy beaches along the east part of the Gold Beach landing zone. But to the west, tall cliffs are cut by small valleys leading to the harbours of Arromanches-les-Bains and Port-en-Bessin, one of the area's favourite holiday resorts.

This mix of coastline posed a problem for the Allies, since many of the beaches were unsuitable for landing. The zone therefore had to extend further: Gold Beach covered 18km, the longest stretch of all five landing zones. It was assigned to the British 2nd Army, whose D-Day objectives were to capture Bayeux and connect with the Americans on Omaha and Canadians at Juno. By nightfall, 25,000 British troops had landed on Gold Beach and pushed the Germans 6 miles inland, at a cost of just 400 casualties. They had reached the outskirts of Bayeux and joined the Canadians, but not the Americans.

Gold Beach was at the heart of the invasion – not just of the beaches and the initial assault, but of the continuous reinforcement and supply effort, through the huge 'Mulberry B' artificial harbour at Arromanches (page 55) and the small 'fuel port' of Port-en-Bessin (page 59). Once the invasion had started, it was also at the heart of decision-making. The commander of all the Allied land forces in Normandy, General Montgomery, set up his first headquarters in this area, 6km inland (page 53); this was only a few hundred metres away from the BBC's temporary radio studio in Château de Creully (page 53), and just over 2km from a large air base at Bazenville, which controlled the tactical air forces in Normandy. And, 8km from the coast, the city of Bayeux became the heart of Free France when General Charles de Gaulle visited on 14 June and declared it to be the first Free French city (page 63).

GETTING THERE AND AROUND

By **car**, the coastal D514 from Ouistreham continues to Ver-sur-Mer (22.5km; 43mins), Asnelles (25.9km; 45mins) and Arromanches-les-Bains

(30km; 50mins), or there are quicker routes if you travel inland. From Cherbourg, the N13 takes you through Bayeux to Gold Beach (114kms; 1hr 32mins). From Cherbourg take the N13 bypassing Bayeux (115km; approx 1hr 28mins).

Bayeux is a convenient base for the Gold Beach sights. If you've taken the **ferry** with your own car (page 5), you can drive to Bayeux from Ouistreham (35km; 43mins), Cherbourg (100km; 1hr 9mins), Le Havre (122km; 1hr 25mins) and Dieppe (218km; 2hrs 33mins). There are fast, direct **trains** from Paris Saint-Lazare to Bayeux (TER 3313; from 2hrs 18mins), or you can change at Caen (2hrs 42mins). From Cherbourg take the TER 3316 to Bayeux (53mins). By **bus** from Bayeux to Ryes, Arromanches, Asnelles, Ver-sur-Mer and Crépon take the Nomad route 121 (approx 1hr). From Caen take the 101 to Asnelles via Douvres-la-Délivrande and coastal towns including Luc-sur-Mer, Saint-Aubin-sur-Mer and Courseulles-sur-Mer. Check the bus routes; days and times can change (w nomad.normandie.fr/lignes-de-cars).

VER-SUR-MER AND AROUND

This quiet little holiday town is not on the beachfront itself but several hundred metres up the hill overlooking the sea, with a fine view. The coastline here was heavily fortified with all the usual obstacles and pillboxes, but the terrain was not as daunting as on other beaches. There was either a low sea wall or barely noticeable sand dunes. This section of Gold Beach was allocated to the 6th and 7th battalions of the Yorkshire Regiment (Green Howards), with the 4th/7th Royal Dragoon Guards and the 8th Armoured Brigade in support. Once across the beach, the 7th Battalion, with Dragoon Guards tanks, fought their way into town, while the 6th Battalion targeted a battery of four 100mm guns on the west side. By noon, the Green Howards had secured Ver-sur-Mer and were on their way south to Crépon. The captured gun battery is close to the site of the new British Normandy Memorial (see below). The Memorial trustees had shortlisted four potential sites, which they put to a vote of 100 D-Day veterans. The spectacular location on the outskirts Ver-sur-Mer won unanimously.

TOURIST INFORMATION

Ver-sur-Mer tourist information office
2 pl de l'Amiral Byrd; 02 31 22 58 58; w tourisme-creully.fr; Jun–Aug 10.00–13.00 & 14.00–18.00 daily, Sep–Oct 10.00–13.00 & 14.00–18.00 Tue–Sun

Creully-sur-Seulles tourist information office 12 pl Edmond Paillaud; 02 31 80 67 08; w tourisme-creully.fr; year-round Mon–Fri, hours vary; check website

WHAT TO SEE AND DO

British Normandy Memorial (Av Paul Poret; w britishnormandymemorial.org; daily; free, although donations appreciated, & €3.50 for all-day parking;) This spectacular new memorial stands high on a hillside just outside Ver-sur-Mer, giving panoramic views over Gold Beach. Opened on 6 June 2021, it comprises a large three-sided monument featuring a 'Wall of Memorial', with cream stone pillars leading off it in a large rectangle surrounded by green lawns. Inscribed on the wall and pillars are the names of the 22,442 servicemen and women who died in Normandy from 6 June to 31 August 1944 (the end of Operation Overlord) serving under British

---

1 The British Normandy Memorial has an incomparable setting. 2 The BBC set up a radio station in the square tower of Château de Creully. ▶

command: the wall lists 1,746 names of those killed on D-Day itself; and names are then presented chronologically on the 160 pillars, running clockwise. Two doorways in the wall lead to a larger-than-life bronze statue of three soldiers rushing ashore.

It was designed by architect Liam O'Connor, who was also behind the Armed Forces Memorial in Staffordshire and the Bomber Command Memorial in London, and involved a long collaboration with the French. The result is one of the most beautiful commemorations of the dead; its perfect symmetry has a wonderful harmony and feeling of grace. Download the app, which guides visitors around the site and can be searched to locate individual names.

America and Gold Beach Museum (2 pl de l'Amiral Byrd; ✆ 02 31 22 58 58; ⓦ goldbeachmusee.fr; ⏱ hours vary, check website; May–Sep 10.00–13.00 & 14.00–18.00 daily; adult/child 5 to 15 years €4.50/2; last admission 30mins before closing) The museum has a name guaranteed to confuse because Gold was a British beach. The explanation is that Ver-sur-Mer had a life before D-Day. *America* was the name of a Fokker tri-motor plane flown by polar explorer Richard E Byrd and three crew on a pioneering non-stop flight across the Atlantic from New York to Paris. They ended up in the surf just off the beach in front of Ver-sur-Mer in the early hours of 1 July 1927. Half of the museum is dedicated to that tale; the other half focuses on the events of 6 June 1944. It's not a large museum so there's no room for big objects like vehicles or artillery. Instead, it makes very good use of annotated maps, photographs, models and small artefacts.

Stanley Hollis hut (Junction of Le Paisty Vert & 69e Brigade Britannique; /// bumble.factories.peppermint) When Company Sergeant Major Stanley Hollis came ashore on this beach with the 6th Battalion, Yorkshire Regiment (Green Howards) at 07.30 on D-Day, he started as he meant to go on. He picked up a Lewis machine gun and emptied a whole drum of ammunition into this hut, which he took to be a German pillbox. However, it wasn't. It was an innocent train stop on the light railway that ran along the beach. No matter. On his way inland and uphill, he rushed two pillboxes (near the new British Normandy Memorial, page 48), single-handedly taking 31 prisoners. Later in the day, in the village of Crépon, he rescued two of his men by storming a machine gun trench. As a result he became the only person to receive the Victoria Cross for actions on D-Day itself. His citation recorded that 'Wherever the fighting was heaviest [he] appeared, displaying the utmost gallantry'.

In his book *The Longest Day*, Cornelius Ryan offered an explanation for what drove Hollis. At the time of the 1940 evacuation at Dunkirk, Hollis had been a despatch rider. Separated from his unit, he took a wrong turn in Lille and came across a hideous massacre. The bodies of over 100 French men, women and children, mown down in a cul-de-sac by German machine guns, were still warm. From then on, Hollis became a merciless hunter of Germans. When he came ashore at Ver-sur-Mer his tally from North Africa and Sicily was over 90, and he intended to increase it.

The small hut was purchased, renovated and dedicated to him by his regiment in 2006. An information board describes his actions, and there's a plinth where visitors leave flowers and stones in memory. He also has an impressive statue in his hometown of Middlesbrough, where he died in 1972.

Memorials A **Sexton 25-pounder self-propelled gun** (SPG, page 138; cnr of rte d'Asnelles/D514 & 69e Brigade Britannique/D112), in brown camouflage, dominates this junction at the northeastern end of Ver-sur-Mer. Next to it is a 'porpoise' – a

steel sled containing extra ammunition that was towed on to the beaches by tanks and SPGs. The Sexton was presented to Ver-sur-Mer by Dr Matthew Kiln, in memory of his father Major Robert Kiln and the British soldiers who landed on this beach. On the opposite side of the junction, where the D514 meets the voie du Débarquement, a tall stone monument commemorates the eight **Royal Artillery regiments of the 50th (Northumbrian) Infantry Division**. Boards in French and English explain the action of each of the regiments as they came ashore on D-Day. During the war, four soldiers of the 50th Division were awarded the Victoria Cross, more than any other division in World War II.

And on the corner between voie du Débarquement and 69e Brigade Britannique towards the beach, the **Ver-sur-Mer liberation monument** commemorates the 2nd Battalion of the Hertfordshire Regiment, under Colonel J R Harper, who garrisoned and managed the bridgehead until 17 August 1944.

Around Ver-sur-Mer

Vera Battery (Just off D112, 450m southeast on 69e Brigade Britannique; /// mystify.snatched.pushing) Here's one for the adventurous as you'll need to find your way through the undergrowth that partially surrounds the bunkers. Vera was a German hilltop inland battery (Widerstandsnest 32) of four 100mm guns in their casemates, with a 10km range that could reach both Gold and Juno beaches. The casemates were heavily bombed in the early hours of D-Day, and then shelled from the sea by the cruiser HMS *Belfast* (now a museum ship by Tower Bridge in London). By the time the Green Howards showed up with two flame-throwing 'Crocodile' tanks later on D-Day, the garrison had had enough and surrendered.

B-3 ALG (Rte de Ver-sur-Mer, between Sainte-Croix-sur-Mer & Ver-sur-Mer; /// demeaning.retaliation.spooned) Surrounded by fields, a low wall marks out three sides of a rectangle, with a rough-hewn stone stele in the centre commemorating the first operations of the Allied air forces based in Europe, while a number of small plaques commemorate the service units working here. The construction of B-3, the first advanced landing ground (page 52), was a tour de force. The Royal Engineers' 24th Airfield Construction Group started work on D-Day itself, and four days later it was operational, complete with a compacted dirt runway, and later a steel mesh runway. Between 10 June and 9 September, four Allied air forces operated from here: RAF 121 Wing (175 squadron), who flew Typhoons, and squadrons from three Spitfire units, 144 Wing (Canada), 135 Wing (New Zealand), and 146 Wing (Rhodesia).

Crépon This small village with its winding streets full of old Normandy fortified manor houses, is 2.5km inland southwest of Ver-sur-Mer. After fighting their way off the beach and through Ver-sur-Mer, the 6th and 7th battalions of the Green Howards, supported by the tanks of the 4th/7th Royal Dragoon Guards, captured Crépon in the afternoon of 6 June, before moving south to Creully-sur-Seulles. The impressive **Green Howards memorial** (cnr of rte d'Arromanches/D65 & pl de l'Église), occupying a small grassy area in the centre of the village, comprises a large statue of a soldier, in a pensive mood, sitting on a pile of rubble, with his helmet dangling from one hand and his rifle in the other. It perfectly captures the look a soldier might have in an after-action moment. Many suggest it's meant to be Stanley Hollis (see opposite). The plaque on the base of the statue does mention him, but the dedication is to the 180 men of the Green Howards who lost their lives on D-Day; they are all named on the wall behind the statue.

At the start of World War II the RAF was a standalone force. The German Luftwaffe's role, working in tandem with its army by using bombers to blast a way through enemy strongpoints for the infantry, was a shock. The RAF quickly developed its own tactical air force and an army–air force command structure in North Africa, which turned the tide in the desert war. One lesson learned was that it was all about airfields, which meant capturing airfields near the frontline. This lesson was adapted for Normandy – if we can't capture airfields quickly (Normandy's largest, Carpiquet on the outskirts of Caen, wasn't captured until 5 July) we must build our own.

From D-Day onwards, teams of specialist US and British engineers rapidly fanned out to scrape out and level runways. They quickly established ammunition stores, fuel stores, landing lights, maintenance areas, defences, control and communication centres, and all the other facilities needed for an airfield. The US Air Force and the RAF had operational Advanced Landing Grounds (ALGs) within a week. American ALGs were prefaced A (eg: A-9), while British and Canadian ALGs were prefaced B.

During the Battle of Normandy, the USAAF and RAF built and operated more than 20 ALGs each. By mid-September 1944, most had been closed and the land handed back to their owners, while the engineers moved further into Europe to build new ALGs. Many ALGs have markers or memorials to their occupants.

Just 500m south along the D65 is another striking piece of artwork. The metal Belgian **Overlord Wings memorial** (cnr of Les Fontaines) depicts two Spitfires and a Hawker Typhoon swooping through the air, in tribute to the Belgian pilots of the 349th (Spitfire), 350th (Spitfire) and 609th (Typhoon) squadrons of the RAF, who flew from B-2 ALG (see above). The fortified farmhouse (now an excellent hotel) opposite was taken over as the HQ for the airfield. The Belgian Air Force commissioned this artwork in 2019, in honour of the 752 Belgians who flew with the RAF in World War II, of whom 207 were killed.

B-2 ALG and Pierre Clostermann stele (5km southwest of Crépon, rue de l'Église, Bazenville, against the churchyard wall) A very stylish stone sculpture in the elliptical shape of a Spitfire wing features two bronze plaques: one is in memory of squadrons 403, 416 and 421 of the Royal Canadian Air Force, who flew from the B-2 ALG between 16 June and 15 August 1944; the other recalls the arrival at this airfield of Pierre Clostermann, a French pilot serving with RAF 602 (City of Glasgow) Squadron, a unit of mixed nationalities flying Spitfires. In June 1944 they were flying daily patrols over Normandy from their base in southern England. However, on 15 June, bad weather was forecast and 602 Squadron was ordered not to return to base but stay overnight at B-2. Thus, Clostermann and two other French pilots (unnamed, but likely to be fellow 602 Squadron pilots J Aubertin and J Remlinger; page 59) became the first Free French aviators to land in France. Behind the sculpture, on the churchyard wall itself, a stainless steel plaque records the fact that the RAF 83rd Group Control Centre for the 2nd Tactical Air Force, responsible for flight control during the Battle of Normandy, was based at Bazenville from 7 June to 10 August 1944.

Ryes CWGC cemetery (D87 near Bazenville, just south of the junction with D112) On a small road and surrounded by open fields, this CWGC cemetery sits relatively undisturbed by traffic. It holds just under 1,000 graves, many of which (652) are British servicemen. There are also 335 Germans and one Pole buried here. Ryes was one of the early permanent cemeteries, receiving its first burials on 8 June 1944.

Creully-sur-Seulles The village and commune of Creully-sur-Seulles were liberated without opposition by the 6th and 7th battalions of the Green Howards, supported by the tanks of the 4th/7th Royal Dragoon Guards, in the evening of D-Day. The village stands on an outcrop overlooking the Seulles River and its centrepiece is the impressive **Château de Creully** (30 pl Edmond Paillaud; 07 89 05 19 12; e e.marie@creully-sur-seulles.fr; w musees-normandie.fr/musees-normandie/chateau-musee-creully; ⊙ guided tours in English & French without reservation 03 Jun–01 Sep 14.00, 15.00, 16.00 & 17.00 Mon; 10.00, 11.00, 14,00, 15.00, 16.00 & 17.00 Tue–Thu; 10.00 & 11.00 Fri; groups can reserve throughout the year; adult/concession/under-18s €6/4/free). The large château, dating back to the 11th century, has been destroyed and rebuilt over time, but despite all that it still looks suitably medieval. The day after D-Day, the BBC moved in and set up a radio station in the square tower. From here, correspondents like Frank Gillard broadcast their vital reports on the invasion and the Battle of Normandy until 21 July 1944. In 1946, the commune became part-owner of the château, which is now used for concerts, exhibitions, conferences, weddings and other events. Tours of the château include the tower and a mock-up of the BBC studio.

Below the château, by the D22, is a handsome stone commemorative wall to the **4th/7th Royal Dragoon Guards**. It features relief sculptures of the Guards' insignia and a tank, as well as lists of the fallen. It also features a poignant quote from Ancient Greek historian Thucydides, used on many war memorials: 'Take these men for your example. Like them, remember that prosperity can only be for the free, that freedom is the sure possession of those alone who have the courage to defend it.' Metal plaques on a stone step in front show the path of the regiment through Normandy.

B-9 ALG (1.5km south of Creully-sur-Seulles on D93 to Lantheuil; /// apple. correlation.snippets) By the side of the road, on the edge of a field, a stone stele with an arched top pays tribute to the pilots who flew from B-9 ALG. B-9 was built by 653rd Road Construction Company of the Royal Engineers' 13th Airfield Construction Group, between 10 and 21 June. It was immediately occupied by

MONTGOMERY'S FIRST HQ IN NORMANDY

General Montgomery established his mobile HQ in the grounds of the Château de Creullet, just outside Creully-sur-Seulles (and not to be confused with the nearby medieval Château de Creully), from 8 to 23 June 1944. The château is a private home and not open to the public, but you can see it from the road. Heading northwest from the château on the D22, just after a small bridge over the Seulles River (/// flumes.advertise.reiterated), you can see the gardens where his mobile HQ was parked, together with the château that appears in the background of so many photographs and newsreel films of Monty.

5

the 143rd Wing of the Royal Canadian Air Force (438, 439 and 440 squadrons), who flew Hawker Typhoons from here until the end of Operation Overlord in late August 1944. A separate grey stone commemorates Typhoon pilot Warrant Officer Carl McConvey, who was killed in an accident while taking off on 16 July 1944.

ASNELLES

This small seaside town, today a place for watersports and relaxation, was a valuable beach for the Allies, since its adjacent low-lying land made it suitable for landings. Just a little further west, the cliffs start, which made things much more difficult. Units of the British 50th (Northumbrian) Infantry Division spread out from here to capture Ryes, Arromanches and Vaux-sur-Aure on the outskirts of Bayeux. On 7 June they entered Bayeux after the Germans withdrew and captured the Longues-sur-Mer Battery. However, the initial landing was not easy. Two Widerstandsnests (page 138) knocked out many tanks and caused heavy casualties; for example, nearly 180 men of the 1st Battalion, Hampshire Regiment, were dead by the evening of D-Day.

There is a **tourist information office** near the beach (cale de l'Essex Yeomanry; \02 31 21 94 02; w tourisme-creully.fr; ⏺ Jul–Aug 10.00–13.00 & 14.00–18.00 daily, but subject to change; check website).

WHAT TO SEE AND DO

Widerstandsnest 37 (Junction of bd de la Mer & 231e Brigade Britannique; by the beachside car park) Built on a tiny headland formed by a kink in the coastline, this German bunker was the perfect place for enfilading fire (page 138) along the beach, in this case from a 75mm gun. Today the bunker is sealed up but, on its side, plaques in French and English tell the story. This gun in particular had caused havoc among the Allied troops and tanks landing here, destroying six tanks on the beach. Eventually Sergeant Robert Palmer of the 8th Armoured (Essex Yeomanry) Brigade, an artillery regiment, was persuaded by his regiment's forward observation officer, whose own unarmed tank had just been hit by the German gun, to have a go at it, even though his thinly armoured Sexton self-propelled gun was hardly up to the task. He realised that the only chance of success was by getting a shell through the main opening of the casemate, which meant getting as close as possible. His driver revved the engine and they roared off at 40mph; when they were just 275m away they lined up and fired. They missed the first time, but their rapid second shot hit their target. It was the last of the Asnelles beach bunkers to be silenced, and Sergeant Palmer was awarded the Military Medal. There are plaques to those who were killed from the **Essex Yeomanry** and also from the **Nottinghamshire (Sherwood Rangers) Yeomanry**, which lost eight Sherman DD (amphibious) tanks as they were landing and a further eight on the beach (six of them to the gun at WN 37). The plaque here says the gun was an 88mm, but it is most likely that it was a World War I French 75mm cannon.

Liberation monument (Cnr of av de la Libération/D514 & rue Devonshire Régiment) Asnelles was captured on 6 June by the 56th Infantry Brigade, part of the 50th (Northumbrian) Infantry Division. All the brigades that landed at Asnelles – the 2nd Battalion, South Wales Borderers; 2nd Battalion, Essex Regiment; and 2nd Battalion, Gloucestershire Regiment – are remembered on this stone monument. One junction west (rue Major Martin) a tall black marble stone also commemorates the 2nd Battalion, South Wales Borderers, who landed here mid-morning in the second wave. By 23.30 they had reached their objective, the bridge at Vaux-sur Aure on the outskirts of Bayeux, and had captured more enemy territory than any other unit in France on 6 June.

ARROMANCHES-LES-BAINS AND AROUND

In 1944, Arromanches-les-Bains was a small fishing village in a steep-sided gully, where the houses were squeezed together into all the available space, separated only by narrow streets. Its capture was assigned to the 1st Battalion of the Royal Hampshire Regiment, who fought their way through Asnelles before walking up on to the plateau on the east side of Arromanches, where they captured the German radar station (the site of the car parks today) at 19.30, before moving down into the town. It wasn't a big battle: Arromanches was in British hands by 22.30. The village may not have been heavily defended, but it was a crucial objective. Within a

MULBERRY HARBOURS

When the Allies started planning the invasion, they believed that the flat-bottomed landing ships needed to deliver the initial assault forces wouldn't be able to deliver the quantity of weapons, vehicles, men, fuel, armaments, food, medicine and equipment required to sustain them in battle. That monumental task would have to be done by ordinary deep-keeled cargo ships, which needed a port. The problem was that it could take weeks to capture a port like Cherbourg and get it operational. It was Winston Churchill, as First Lord of the Admiralty, who in 1917, during World War I, had first come up with the concept of constructing an artificial harbour for landing supplies. It was not taken up, but in 1943 after the 1942 Dieppe Raid had demonstrated the need for invading forces to be quickly resupplied, the concept was enthusiastically embraced by Operation Overlord planners. The process started on 7 June by building breakwaters to create sheltered water off all five beaches; these would be incorporated into full-facility artificial harbours at Saint-Laurent-sur-Mer (Omaha) and Arromanches (Gold). Everything had a codename. The sheltered waters ('gooseberries') off Sword, Juno and Utah were created using floating 'bombardons' (61m cross-shaped concrete and steel tubes) and 'corncobs' (scuttled ships). The harbours ('mulberries') created by these breakwaters were reinforced with 146 colossal 2,459–7,470-tonne concrete caissons ('phoenixes'), which acted as harbour walls, with defensive AA guns and barrage balloons. Inside the harbours there were deep-water wharves ('spuds') for ships to unload 1.5km offshore, with floating roadways ('whales') on pontoons ('beetles') to take the vehicles and supplies ashore. Other types of pier catered for different cargoes and different ships.

On 19 June, just as the two mulberries were operational, the worst storm in 40 years swept in. It damaged Mulberry B at Arromanches-les-Bains and, potentially more seriously, destroyed Mulberry A at Omaha. But as it turns out, this was not disastrous. The Americans were forced to resort back to landing everything directly on to Omaha Beach. Once they improved the efficiency of the process, they began to outstrip the tonnage passing through Mulberry B on Gold Beach. Ironically, given the time and expense, the Allies may not have needed the artificial harbours at all.

5

fortnight it had become the hub of the huge artificial harbour known as 'Mulberry B' (page 55), or 'Port Winston' as it was nicknamed by the troops. Suddenly those narrow streets had to cope with an average of 6,874 tonnes of supplies coming ashore every day, not to mention hundreds of vehicles and men. Today it is still a small village with narrow streets, crammed in between the slopes, which is why a visit to Arromanches comes in two parts: the hilltop and the town. Explore the impressive (and busy) viewpoints and markers before walking down to the D-Day Landing Museum and the beach. There is a **tourist information office** in the town centre (2 rue Maréchal Joffre; \02 31 22 36 45; w bayeux-bessin-tourisme.com; ⊕ Nov–Mar 14.30–17.30 Sat, Sun & French school hols; Apr–Jun & Sep–Oct 10.00–13.00 & 14.00–18.00 daily; Jul–Aug 09.00–19.00 Mon–Sat, 10.00–13.00 & 14.00–19.00 Sun & public hols).

WHAT TO SEE AND DO

The hilltop Built on a former gun emplacement at the top of the cliffs, the **Mulberry Harbour viewing platform** (rue du Calvaire, just off D514) has spectacular panoramic views over the remains of Mulberry B, with information panels indicating what you are looking at.

There is a string of worthwhile sights as you head west along the rue du Calvaire from the viewing platform, back towards the town.

First, less than 100m away, is the **Royal Engineers memorial**. Standing in front of two of Allan Beckett's 24m 'whale' roadway bridging spans (page 55), a plaque on a tall column summarises the hugely impressive contribution the 87,000 Royal Engineers in Normandy made to the invasion. They did pretty much anything that required construction, and a bit of destruction too: from secretly reconnoitring the landing beaches and drawing up maps in advance of D-Day, to landing with airborne troops to dismantle charges on bridges, to building Mulberry harbours, airfields, roads and water supplies.

Across the road is the **D-Day 75 memorial garden**, an evocative artwork of young soldiers wading ashore on D-Day through waves and obstacles. The life-size figures are made from metal washers welded together and have an ephemeral quality. There is a sandstone statue of D-Day veteran Bill Pendell sitting with his beret and medals, opposite another statue showing his 22-year-old self. Bill, an 11th Armoured Division veteran, was chosen to represent D-Day veterans by D-Day Revisited as an ordinary soldier. Sadly he died, aged 97, six months before the garden was unveiled. It was created by John Everiss at the Royal Hospital Chelsea for the 2019 RHS Chelsea Flower Show, and was then gifted to Arromanches in a ceremony on 6 June 2019.

At the end of rue du Calvaire, as it begins to dip down the hill towards the town, is **Arromanches 360°** (\02 31 06 06 45; w arromanches360.com; ⊕ 30 Jan–Mar & Oct 10.00–17.00 daily, Apr–Aug 10.00–18.00 daily, Sep 10.00–17.30 daily, Nov–6 Jan 10.00–17.00 Tue–Sun; adult/concession/under-10s €7/6/free). This in-the-round cinema shows a documentary film, *The 100 Days of the Battle of Normandy*, which gives a useful overview of the battle using British, Canadian, German, American and French archives.

On the walk down into town on rue Charles Laurent, a **75mm Sherman tank** (/// settlements.collision.uneven) is parked on what looks like a terrace, but is

◀ 1 The impressive remains of the Mulberry B Harbour at Gold Beach. 2 The statue of D-Day veteran Bill Pendell in Arromanches's memorial garden. 3 & 4 'Beetle' pontoons were used to build floating roadways – and you can still find large remnants of them in Arromanches.

ctually the roof of German gun emplacement **Widerstandsnest 43**. This particular tank was used by the French Army after the war and then became a memorial to all those who fought in and around Arromanches.

The town

D-Day Landing Museum
(Musée du Débarquement, pl du 6 Juin; ☎02 31 22 34 31; w musee-arromanches.fr; ⏰ Feb–Dec daily, hours vary, check website; adult/child €12.70/8.20) The first museum in Normandy to commemorate D-Day and the Battle of Normandy opened on this site in 1954. The current building, opened on 1 April 2023, is bigger and very well organised, telling the story of the invasion and, in particular, of the artificial harbour right in front of it. Its displays are more technically advanced and it offers an 8-minute video summary of the invasion and the Mulberry project in a new cinema. But it also retains some of the old museum's most popular exhibits, especially the huge, moving model of Mulberry B. A rooftop viewing platform, scheduled to open in 2024, should offer panoramic views over the harbour.

Liberators Museum – Normandy 44
(9 rue Col René Michel, ☎02 14 08 60 98; f; ⏰ Apr–mid-Sep 09.00–18.00 daily; adult/child aged 10–15/under-10 €4/2.50/free; guided tours on request) This small museum is stuffed with personal items, uniforms, badges, documents and photographs donated by veterans.

Allan Beckett memorial
(Cale Maréchal Montgomery, beside the ramp down to the beach) A stone plinth honours Major Allan Beckett, the Royal Engineer who designed the 'whale' floating roadway, a crucial component of Mulberry harbours. Prime Minister Winston Churchill had taken a keen interest in the harbour and wrote a memo: 'Piers for use on beaches: they must float up and down with the tide. The anchor problem must be mastered – let me have the best solution worked out. Don't argue the matter. The difficulties will argue for themselves.' It was Beckett who came up with articulated bridge spans, floating on 'beetle' pontoons and held in place with a new kind of 'kite' anchor with flat blades, quite unlike the traditional kedge anchor with hooks. The plinth has one of these anchors on top, and alongside is one of his 24m bridge spans, while some of his 'beetles' still litter the beach just 100m away.

Around Arromanches-les-Bains

Mulberry Harbour 'whale' bridge
(D514, close to the junction with D516, opposite Camping Les Bas Carreaux; /// trooping.grows.recommend) One of the

---

DON'T LOOK UP!

The D-Day Landing Museum (see above) has a copy of a famous aerial photograph. At 16.30 on 2 August 1944, as the Allies at Mulberry B were busy unloading the vast quantities of war materials needed to break out of Normandy into the rest of France, they were being photographed… by a German pilot. Luftwaffe pilot Erich Sommer was flying the world's first combat mission by a jet photo-reconnaissance aircraft, the Arado 234. Erich had designed a rearward-facing periscope that he could use to check he wasn't leaving a vapour trail, which would draw attention to his presence. He wasn't – not that it mattered much. Few enemy aircraft and no AA guns could reach him at 11,000m, and travelling at 800km/h.

24m 'whale' vehicle bridge spans from Mulberry B (page 55) sits beside the main road. Two more sections in a field nearby might get added to this one.

Longues-sur-Mer Battery (D104, 39 rue de la Mer, signposted from D514)
The coastal artillery battery at Longues-sur-Mer is one of the most popular D-Day battlefield sites to visit: it's in the midst of the landing beaches; it's an open site, free to visit at any time; and it is mostly intact, with its guns and bunkers standing on the cliff edge. The battery comprised four Czech-made (Skoda) 150mm naval guns in a line of casemates, plus a 120mm ex-Russian field gun on an open emplacement (no longer there), as well as defence trenches, mortar pits, tobruk machine gun positions and AA gun positions, all within a ring of barbed wire and mines. On D-Day it exchanged fire with naval ships, notably the light cruiser HMS *Ajax* (already famous for her part in the Battle of the River Plate, when she and two other Royal Navy cruisers (HMS *Exeter* and HMS *Achilles*) attacked and then blockaded the German pocket battleship *Graf Spee* in December 1939; trapped in Montevideo, *Graf Spee* eventually scuttled herself), 11km away off Gold Beach, and the battleship USS *Arkansas*, off Omaha. Casemate no 4 (the easternmost, next to the car park) was silenced for a few hours in the morning and the communications link with the control bunker was severed, causing the whole battery to slow its rate of fire. By the evening all but one gun had been put out of action. On 7 June, after a bombing raid overnight, the 120-strong garrison (half of them over 40 years old) quickly surrendered to the British 2nd Devonshire Regiment, who had landed at Asnelles and worked their way around the back of Arromanches to Longues-sur-Mer.

Casemate no 4 has been shattered, though not on D-Day and not intentionally. Between 18 and 21 June the British built B-11 ALG on the flat clifftop east of the battery. The engineers put a pair of 40mm anti-aircraft guns on the roof of casemate no 4 and stored ordnance inside. On the night of 6 July somebody was allegedly careless with a cigarette; there was a colossal explosion and the whole bunker was ripped apart, killing four servicemen. A polished black marble marker for the **B-11 ALG**, beside the tourist information office building by the battery car park (/// murals.solids.torchlight), records that between 21 June and 4 September 1944, Free French pilots Pierre Clostermann (page 52), J Aubertin and J Remlinger were based here with the RAF 602 City of Glasgow Squadron.

Longues-sur-Mer Battery can get very busy with schools and tour groups, especially on weekdays in the summer. If you visit early in the morning or in the evening you'll get the best light, and will have the place almost to yourself.

PORT-EN-BESSIN

This picturesque fishing port is popular with tourists during the summer, with its old streets and plenty of cafés and restaurants. In 1944, it was popular with the Allies as one of the key gateways for supplies. It was particularly important for fuel: the port was the onshore terminal for PLUTO Minor fuel pipelines (page 60).

If the road that runs beside the port (quai Félix Faure) looks familiar, it's due to the long tracking shot in the movie *The Longest Day* (page 24). The action when Kieffer and his commandos storm the casino in Ouistreham was actually shot here. But it's the wrong way round: the commandos are not heading inland along the quay, they are fighting their way towards the harbour. The real troops of 47 (Royal Marine) Commando landed at Asnelles on D-Day and made their way, suffering losses en route, to the outskirts of Port-en-Bessin. They attacked on 7 June and, in

The codename PLUTO can be misleading. Although the headline component of Operation PLUTO was establishing underwater pipelines, the operation was really about establishing a network of fuel and oil pipelines both under the sea and on land, right up to the point of use.

PLUTO Major was an amazing piece of conceptual and practical engineering – but didn't quite meet expectations. Ten 8cm-diameter pipes would carry fuel and oil at high pressure from disguised pumping stations at Shanklin on the Isle of Wight, 130km across the English Channel to Querqueville on the outskirts of Cherbourg, from where the pipeline would continue to the battlefront. The Shanklin–Cherbourg pipelines, having been slowly unrolled from giant floating reels fabulously named 'conundrums' towed behind ships, were intended to deliver 3,550 metric tonnes of fuel a day and were expected to be operational sometime after June 18. In the event, they only became operational on 22 September and stopped working ten days later, by which time they had delivered a total of 3,350 tonnes, less than the target for one day.

PLUTO Minor was less glamorous, but designed to be operational much earlier. Work started on these pipelines on 9 June. They ran 4km inland to fuel dumps at Le Mont Cauvin, from the quayside at Port-en-Bessin and from floating pipes ('tombolas') that extended a kilometre out to sea from the beach at Sainte-Honorine-des-Pertes, 3km to the west. Medium-size tankers connected to the pipeline at Port-en-Bessin and to the Tombola buoys at Sainte-Honorine-des Pertes to discharge their cargo from 16 June. The system remained operational until 10 October 1944 when the Allies reached Antwerp.

a fierce battle against hardened defenders, they finally got the upper hand in the evening. The German garrison finally surrendered at 04.00 on 8 June.

There is a **tourist information office** right by the port (quai Baron Gérard; 02 31 22 45 80; w bayeux-bessin-tourisme.com; Apr–Jun & Sep–Oct 10.00–13.00 & 14.00–18.00 daily; Jul–Aug 09.00–19.00 Mon–Sat, 10.00–13.00 & 14.00–19.00 Sun & bank hols; Nov–Mar 10.00–13.00 Sat–Sun).

WHAT TO SEE AND DO
Museum of Underwater Wrecks
(Musée des Épaves Sous-Marines du Débarquement, D6 to Escures; 02 31 21 17 06; w calvados-tourisme.co.uk/offer/museum-of-underwater-wrecks; Jun–Sep 10.00–noon & 14.00–19.00 Sun–Fri; adult/child €8/5; May 10.00–noon & 14.00–19.00 weekends & public hols) This museum features a collection of, for the most part, rusted vehicles, guns and other pieces of equipment fished up from the sea off the landing beaches of Normandy.

Memorials
Unveiled on the 60th anniversary of D-Day (2004), a **commemoration stone** by the harbourside (rue du Castel; /// schematic.compositions.symptom) is engraved with images of tankers, barrage balloons, pipelines and jerrycans, highlighting the critical role Port-en-Bessin played for tankers carrying fuel

1 The formidable coastal battery at Longues-sur-Mer. 2 Graves of unknown sailors in Bayeux CWGC cemetery. ▶

in the early days of the invasion. On the car park wall 20m away (/// fearful. tomato.nationality) a small circular plaque commemorates the 47 (Royal Marine) Commando troops who captured Port-en-Bessin.

If you're prepared to walk out to the end of the harbour's east mole, one of Normandy's ten **signal monuments** (page 138) stands there, guarding the harbour entrance along with the local fishermen. It doesn't look particularly big from the shore, but it is actually 4.3m tall. On the east hill overlooking the town, a simple stone plinth (/// governed.sublet.misted) honours **Captain Terence 'Freddie' Cousins** of 47 Commando, who led a successful assault up the hill to the German bunkers and trenches at the top on 7 June, helping to bring about the capture of Port-en-Bessin. He was killed by a hand grenade in the process and is buried in Bayeux's CWGC cemetery. Cousins was nominated for a Victoria Cross, although it was declined somewhere up the chain of command, but he did receive a posthumous mention in despatches.

On the west hill is a memorial to **47 Commando** (Le Sémaphore, at a viewpoint on a short footpath from the road; /// poky.jovially.fidgeted), who liberated the port on 8 June. The spot is well worth visiting for the spectacular view of the port and town.

BAYEUX

The medieval city of Bayeux, just 7km from the coast, was lucky – its quick, uncontested capture, after the Germans fled, on 7 June meant that its half-timbered houses, cathedral and other old buildings avoided the destruction that befell other Normandy cities. (The world-famous Bayeux Tapestry depicting William the Conqueror's invasion of England in 1066 had been taken to a secret underground shelter in the Château de Sourches, in the Sarthe département in Pays de la Loire.)

A week later, on 14 June, General Charles de Gaulle (see opposite) arrived in the narrow cobbled streets and declared the city to be the first Free French city. But there was a snag: those intact streets were too narrow for most military vehicles, so the Royal Engineers and Royal Pioneer Corps quickly had to build a ring-road around the city centre, which is where Bayeux's World War II monuments and memorials are to be found today.

Though only 35km apart, the gap between Bayeux's liberation and Saint-Lô's on 19 July, 42 days later, highlights the difficulties the Allied forces faced as they tried to advance among the hedgerows of the bocage.

Bayeux's **tourist information office** can be found right in the centre (rue Saint Jean; ⟍ 02 31 51 28 28; w bayeux-bessin-tourisme.com; ⊕ Apr–Jun & Sep–Oct 10.00–13.00 & 14.00–18.00 daily, Jul–Aug 09.00–19.00 daily; Nov–Mar 09.30–12.30 & 14.00–17.30 daily; closed 25 Dec & 1 Jan).

WHAT TO SEE AND DO
Memorial Museum of the Battle of Normandy (Musée Mémorial Bataille de Normandie, bd Fabian Ware; ⟍ 02 31 51 25 50; w bayeuxmuseum.com/en/memorial-museum-battle-of-normandy; ⊕ Feb–Apr & Oct–Dec 10.00–12.30 & 14.00–18.00 daily, May–Sep 09.30–18.30 daily; last entry 45mins before closing; adult/child €7.50/5.50) This extensive museum tells the story of the Battle of Normandy from a French perspective, using plenty of information panels and historic photographs. It also has a large collection of military vehicles and equipment both inside and outside in the grounds. Don't miss the documentary

Charles de Gaulle was born in Lille in 1890, and joined an infantry regiment as a 2nd lieutenant in 1913. In World War I he was wounded three times, mentioned in despatches three times and captured by the Germans at Verdun. In the interwar years, de Gaulle became a vocal proponent of mechanised warfare, lobbying for the adoption of tank divisions.

When, in World War II, the Germans swept into Belgium and France, de Gaulle was commanding the 4th Tank Division. He put up stubborn resistance to the rapid German advance at Verdun (once again) and was promoted to brigadier general. His military expertise had already brought him to the attention of the French government and, in early June 1940, as France was beginning to collapse in the face of the German 'blitzkrieg', Prime Minister Paul Reynaud appointed de Gaulle under-secretary of state for national defence and war, and sent him to London to meet Prime Minister Winston Churchill. A week later, when France finally fell to the Germans, de Gaulle refused to countenance surrender and escaped back to London, from where he made his historic 'Appel du 18 Juin' broadcast, urging his countrymen to continue the fight against Nazi occupation. His impassioned plea ignited the flames of resistance, and he became the de facto leader of the Free French Forces in exile.

When the Normandy invasion took place in June 1944, his Free French soldiers, airmen and sailors were able to be a part of it, and on 14 June de Gaulle himself stepped ashore in Normandy. One of the first things he did was drive to Bayeux, where he set up the first Free French administration on French soil, and, to great applause, declared it the first Free French city in France.

De Gaulle's vision extended beyond the battlefield. He tirelessly championed the restoration of French independence and self-determination, culminating in his appointment as provisional president of France in 1944, a position he held until 1946. After the war, he played a pivotal role in shaping the new French Republic. His leadership as Prime Minister in 1958 and then President of France from 1959 to 1969 was instrumental in establishing France as a major power on the world stage, and his legacy continues to resonate today. He died in 1970.

General de Gaulle in Bayeux on 14 June 1944.

Gold Beach and Bayeux **BAYEUX**

5

ASSOCIATED PRESS/A

on Operation Overlord in the cinema and the section devoted to the war correspondents of World War II.

In the grounds there are three commemorative stones: two are dedicated to fallen soldiers from the regiments that liberated Bayeux, the **2nd Battalion, Essex Regiment** and the **Nottinghamshire (Sherwood Rangers) Yeomanry**; the third is dedicated to members of the **Corps of Military Police** who gave their lives in Normandy and beyond.

Just outside the grounds, across the rue des Cordeliers near the junction with the D5, is a simple headstone commemorating **war photographer Robert Capa**, 'taker of legendary photos of the landings', as the inscription says. It is by the start of the **Reporters Memorial Trail**, an inspiring route through the woods to a small and tranquil park (which you can also access from rue de Verdun). The 300m-long path runs between pairs of tall stone steles inscribed with the names of over 2,000 journalists who have been killed or gone missing, year by year. The steles covering the World War II years are closest to the park. Inevitably, the number of markers is continuously growing. Each year a ceremony is held to coincide with the Bayeux-Calvados-Normandy Award for war correspondents, at which the latest stele is unveiled. With no space left on the original path, a second path now branches off and runs parallel to it.

CWGC cemetery
(1945 bd Fabian Ware; ♿) The largest CWGC cemetery in Normandy holds the graves of 4,100 Commonwealth servicemen, plus 500 graves of other nations, including Germans. It's an impressive site, with a large stone in the middle inscribed: 'Their name liveth for evermore.' There are always small personal wreaths and poppies placed at its base. Rank upon rank of graves stretch out on either side of the cemetery. The Allies set up a number of military surgical hospitals in Bayeux and many of those buried here came from those medical units. One Victoria Cross recipient lies here: Corporal Sidney Bates of the Royal Norfolk Regiment responded to a heavy attack on his company, near Sourdeval on 8 August, by charging at the enemy, firing a light machine gun from his hip. He was hit twice but each time he got back up and moved forward. He was hit a third time but kept firing until the enemy withdrew. He died soon after from his wounds.

Bayeux Memorial
(1939 bd Fabian Ware; opposite the CWGC cemetery) This 50m-tall neoclassical carved stone monument, with two grand porticos separated by a colonnade, stands opposite the Bayeux cemetery. It was designed by Philip Hepworth, the CWGC principal architect for northwest Europe, who was also behind cemeteries including Ranville (page 19) and the Canadian one at Bény-sur-Mer (page 44). It commemorates almost 1,800 Commonwealth servicemen killed during the Overlord campaign who, poignantly, have no known grave.

General Eisenhower statue
(Eisenhower roundabout, at the junction of D613 & D572) A larger-than-life-size bronze statue of General Eisenhower (page 82) in battledress with his hands on his hips stands on a small plinth, with a ceremonial arch behind him. He's not easy to visit – this is a busy roundabout – so it may be best just to honour him with a salute as you drive past.

6

Omaha Beach and Around Pointe du Hoc

Of all the D-Day beaches, Omaha has the most fearsome reputation. Standing on the beach today and looking up at the bluffs, which in June 1944 were bristling with defences, it's easy to understand how terrifying it must have been for the young American troops who came ashore here, and to understand why the casualty rate on D-Day (2,400 killed or wounded) was so high. Soldiers on the other D-Day beaches had towns or sand dunes to assault, while Omaha had steep hills. The daunting task of getting ashore, climbing those hills and overwhelming the enemy was given to the US Army's V Corp, comprising the 1st and 29th infantry divisions and the US Rangers. The 1st Division took on the formidable fortifications at the beach's eastern end, while the 29th tackled the no less formidable defences to the west. It was a horror show. Many landing craft got caught on obstacles on the way to the beach or came ashore in the wrong places; nearly all their amphibious tanks sank before reaching the beach; and the withering fire directed at them was greater than anyone had expected. At one point, General Omar Bradley (page 71), in charge of all the US troops heading for Omaha and Utah, considered giving up at Omaha and withdrawing.

The gun battery to the west on the cliffs at Pointe du Hoc was the early-morning target of the US 2nd Ranger Battalion, who heroically scaled the cliffs and captured the battery, only to find the guns were missing. Instead, the closest artillery threat on this side came from Grandcamp-Maisy, almost 6km further west, where there was another German battery, which was buried after its capture and remained hidden until 2004. Today, the 6km-long beach is popular during the summer months with locals and holidaymakers, who share it with D-Day history explorers. There is a promenade road that runs along the edge of the beach from the eastern Saint-Laurent Draw (page 71) to the Vierville Draw (page 73) at the west end. Summer homes and guest houses lie behind it. If you pack a towel and an umbrella for shade, you can take time out from D-Day touring and chill out on the beach for a while, thinking about what an extraordinary contrast your experience is with that of those young men 80 years ago on the same spot.

There are some important sites to visit in the area – Pointe du Hoc and the American Cemetery being the most popular – along with good museums and plenty of bunkers and memorials.

GETTING THERE AND AROUND

By **car** from Ouistreham, take the N13 to Caen, then bypass Bayeux to reach Omaha Beach (65km; 45mins–1hr). If you have time, take the much longer coastal D514

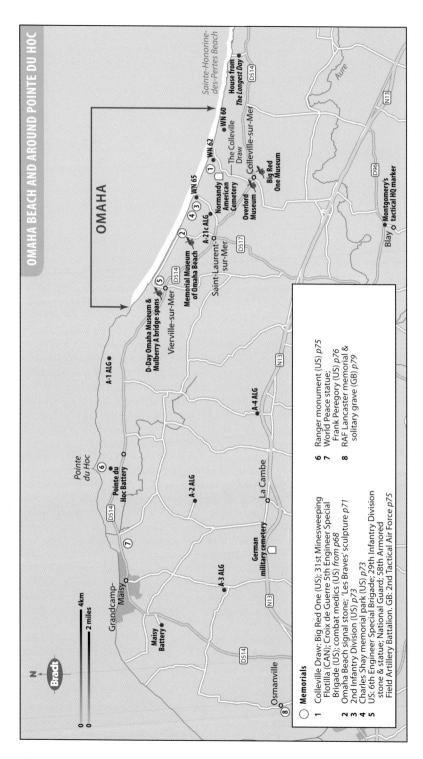

OMAHA

Sainte-Honorine-des-Pertes Beach

House from *The Longest Day*

D514

Aure

N13

WN 60

WN 62

The Colleville
Draw

① Normandy
American
Cemetery

Colleville-sur-Mer

Big Red
One Museum

WN 65

④ ③

② A-21c ALG

Overlord
Museum

D96

Saint-Laurent-
sur-Mer

D517

Memorial Museum
of Omaha Beach

Blay ○ Montgomery's
tactical HQ marker

D514

⑤

Vierville-sur-Mer

D-Day Omaha Museum &
Mulberry A bridge spans

A-1 ALG

N13

A-4 ALG

*Pointe
du Hoc*

⑥

**Pointe du
Hoc Battery** ○

A-2 ALG

D514

⑦

La Cambe ○

**German
military cemetery**

N13

Grand-
camp-
Maisy ○

A-3 ALG

**Maisy
Battery** ●

D514

Osmanville

⑧

N

Bradt

0 ——— 4km
0 ——— 2 miles

Memorials

○

1 Colleville Draw: Big Red One (US); 31st Minesweeping
   Flotilla (CAN); Croix de Guerre 5th Engineer Special
   Brigade (US); combat medics (US) *from p68*
2 Omaha Beach signal stone; 'Les Braves' sculpture *p71*
3 2nd Infantry Division (US) *p73*
4 Charles Shay memorial park (US) *p73*
5 US: 6th Engineer Special Brigade; 29th Infantry Division
   stone & statue; National Guard; 58th Armored
   Field Artillery Battalion. GB: 2nd Tactical Air Force *p75*

6 Ranger monument (US) *p75*
7 World Peace statue;
   Frank Peregory (US) *p76*
8 RAF Lancaster memorial &
   solitary grave (GB) *p79*

66

(58km; 1½–2hrs). To get to Pointe du Hoc, continue west from Colleville-sur-Mer through Saint-Laurent-sur-Mer and Vierville-sur-Mer (10km; approx 18mins). By car from Cherbourg, also take the N13, but southbound through the Cotentin Peninsula sites (90km; approx 1hr 6mins).

By public transport, take the TER **train** to Bayeux (from 1hr 13mins), and then the Nomad 120 **bus** (4/day Mon–Sat) onwards to Port-en-Bessin, Colleville-sur-Mer, St Laurent-sur-Mer, Vierville-sur-Mer and Grandcamp Maisy.

The area is possible to visit by **bike**, but there are hills to negotiate. Otherwise take a car or **tour**.

COLLEVILLE-SUR-MER AND AROUND

The small village of Colleville-sur-Mer, which marks the eastern end of Omaha Beach, stretches from the sea up the hill behind, where a 19th-century washhouse gives an echo of the past, along with a church that was partly destroyed during the invasion and rebuilt. Set back from the hills overlooking the beach, the village was damaged by shelling and bombing, but didn't play any defensive role. At the end of D-Day it was just overrun by US troops heading inland as fast as they could. Today it's the site of the Normandy American Cemetery and the memorials around, which make the commune so well known.

TOURIST INFORMATION

Isigny-sur-Mer tourist information office 16 Rue Emile Demagny; 02 31 21 46 00; w isigny-omaha-tourisme.fr; hours vary, but often 09.30–12.30 & 14.00–18.00; check website. This is the bigger tourist office, with good facilities, bike hire & hotel bookings.

Isingy Omaha tourist information office Lotissement Omaha Centre, near the car park for the Overlord Museum, Colleville-sur-Mer; 02 31 21 46 00; w isigny-omaha-tourisme.fr; hours vary; check website. This is a very small tourist office with basic information & brochures.

WHAT TO SEE AND DO

Normandy American Cemetery (Rte du Cimètiere Americain; 02 31 51 62 00; w abmc.gov/Normandy; Apr–Sep 09.00–18.00 daily, Oct–Mar 09.00–17.00 daily;) On a hill above Omaha Beach, this vast cemetery, covering 70ha, is one of the most visited sites on the D-Day landing beaches, and with good reason. However busy it seems to be, the site is so big and so well laid out that you can always find a peaceful spot for quiet reflection. By the visitor centre are large panels and a short film (in English) telling the personal and moving stories of some of those buried here. Paths shaded by tall trees, with a view of the beach below, lead to the main cemetery, where 9,387 graves stretch out. Two memorials mark the near and far boundaries. The first one you arrive at has maps and details of the landings and a monumental bronze statue of a man lifting his hands and eyes to the sky, called 'The Spirit of American Youth Rising from the Waves', while two granite statues at the far end represent France and the United States. The grave of Theodore Roosevelt Jr, son of President Theodore Roosevelt (page 87), is here. Also buried here are the two highest-ranking Americans killed in friendly fire on 25 July 1944 at Saint-Lô: General Lesley J McNair and Major Thomas D Howie (page 109). There are 45 sets of brothers, most buried side by side, including Preston and Robert Niland, whose story inspired the 1998 film *Saving Private Ryan*. There is a chapel and a peaceful garden of remembrance, where 1,557 names on the 'Walls of the Missing' remember those whose bodies were initially not found; bronze rosettes by some of the names show those who have

6

been recovered and identified. Even today, more bodies are found and identified, giving hope to the families of the lost.

The Colleville Draw Immediately to the east of the Normandy American Cemetery is the Colleville Draw, one of the vital exit valleys from the beach (page 137), where there are a number of important sites. These are accessible only on foot – but that gives you some sense of the task faced by the exhausted soldiers of the US 1st Infantry Division. To reach it, there is a footpath from the cemetery just east of the car park (starting at /// criminally.pitches.slashed) or paths from the lower beach car parks (starting at /// coast.ceases.scruff & scrambles.sunniest.pity).

Widerstandsnest 62 The path passes through the extensive German bunkers and trenches of WN 62. In the middle of the 'resistance nest' is the command bunker (/// clubhouses.folded.tabloid) where Oberleutnant Bernhard Frerking, of the 352nd Infantry Division, spent much of D-Day directing artillery fire on to the beach while, at the same time, trying to reach his missing commander at WN 59, Major Werner Pluskat (page 70). Frerking was shot and killed while trying to retreat with his men. He is buried in La Cambe German cemetery (page 78). By the bunker is a detailed map of the defences, with details of the spot where the flame-throwers were positioned, next to the anti-tank ditches, and where Heinrich Severloh (see below) fired from (to the right of you, looking towards the sea), before being forced to retreat on June 7.

Big Red One memorial (/// cooperating.comparisons.credible) The tribute to the US 1st Infantry Division (nicknamed Big Red One because of their uniform's shoulder patch) is an 8.5m-tall, six-sided obelisk inscribed with the names of those 627 soldiers from the division who died assaulting Omaha Beach. Stone benches around the base enable visitors to sit and contemplate what went on in this place. Just uphill to the south is a granite lectern with a summary of the Big Red One's struggle to get ashore. By the end of the day, they had secured a beachhead 2.5km deep. Over the next week they fought their way 37km south and captured the high ground around Caumont-sur-Aure. Medals of Honor for conspicuous heroism were awarded to three men for their actions on D-Day, and to another two for their actions four days later near the villages of Goville and Vaubadon. On the back of the lectern's pedestal there is a small stainless steel plaque to Private 1st Class Manuel Otero Martinez, of the 1st Infantry Division, who was the only person from Spain and Galicia to die at Omaha on D-Day. It was placed there by the Military History Museum of A Coruña, the city in which he was born.

THE BEAST OF OMAHA

Heinrich Severloh was Oberleutnant Bernhard Frerking's orderly. While Frerking directed artillery fire from Widerstandsnest 62, Severloh manned an MG 42 machine gun in front of the command bunker. He claimed to have fired over 13,500 rounds with the machine gun and 400 with his rifles, after which he escaped to Colleville, where he was captured. In a 2004 interview, Severloh, who has also written a book about his experiences, claimed he had shot 'at least 1,000 men, most likely more than 2,000', adding: 'But I do not know how many men I shot. It was awful. Thinking about it makes me want to throw up.'

31st Canadian Minesweeping Flotilla memorial (/// redo.journeying. ceremonial) A little further down the hill, another granite lectern commemorates the work of the minesweepers in clearing the way for the invasion fleet, in particular the 31st Canadian Flotilla who, just after midnight on 6 June, started clearing the assault path. Using electronic navigation aids, they had to steer a precise and constant course, towing cables to cut tethered mines, within the range of the German batteries, and in moonlight. Amazingly, they weren't detected.

Croix de Guerre 5th Engineer Special Brigade (/// pierces.wildly.birthday) The Croix de Guerre is a French military decoration awarded to French or Allied soldiers for gallantry. This monument represents the Croix de Guerre awarded to the whole unit of the US 5th Engineer Special Brigade on 25 May 1945, 17 days after VE Day, for exceptional services in the liberation of France. It takes the form of a 3.6m-high, four-sided stone obelisk sitting on the roof of a German casemate that housed a 7.5cm field gun. There are plaques listing components of the brigade, including the combat demolition teams who came ashore in the first wave. Engineer special brigades were responsible for managing the beach. At the start, that involved blowing up obstacles while under fire; once the beach had been secured, it meant clearing roads, building bridges and ramps, towing vehicles and generally making sure every soldier and vehicle could get on to and off the beach as efficiently as possible. As the days and weeks passed, it took on a sort of port authority role.

Combat medics memorial (/// intruded.insight.realness) Down on the beach, on a large rock that is sometimes submerged, depending on the tide, there is a bronze plaque to the combat medics of the 16th Infantry Regiment, 1st Infantry Division. This very rock afforded the medics, and their patients, a little protection from the direct fire from WN 62 (see opposite), though none from artillery and mortar fire dropping behind them.

Overlord Museum (Lotissement Omaha Center; ☎ 02 31 22 00 55; w overlordmuseum.com; ◷ Feb–Mar & Oct–Dec 10.00–17.30 daily, Apr–May & Sep 10.00–18.30 daily, Jun–Aug 09.30–19.00 daily, last entry 1hr before closing; adult/child €9.50/7) Just off the main D514 road through Colleville, 2km inland from the American Cemetery (page 67), this is one of Normandy's larger museums. Its modern, warehouse-style building houses an extensive collection of vehicles (many of them German), weapons and other pieces of equipment. There are large and effective dioramas, such as a German two-ton truck on a street setting in Falaise, exactly mirroring a 1944 black-and-white photo of the real scene. There are some rare items here, including a huge artillery tractor, a remote-controlled bomb-delivery vehicle and, for real enthusiasts, a German engineer regiment's 16-ton gantry for maintaining tanks in the field – one of only two that still exist. A recent, poignant, addition to the museum is a photo gallery of veterans, with their personal accounts and recollections.

Big Red One Museum (Rte d'Omaha Beach/D514; ☎ 02 31 21 53 81; ⓕ; ◷ Apr–Sep 10.00–18.00 daily; Oct–Mar 10.00–12.30 & 14.00–18.00 daily; adult/under-12s €5/free) Around the corner from the Overlord Museum, this museum is small but interesting, especially if you get a chance to engage with the enthusiastic owner. Pierre-Louis Gosselin has been collecting D-Day objects and memorabilia since he was nine. He has a close relationship with the Big Red One (US 1st Infantry Division) veterans association and has collected many personal items and stories

6

from soldiers and their families in the USA. He still goes down to the beach at low tide to look for artefacts and takes tour groups down there.

East of Colleville-sur-Mer Where the beach ends and the cliffs continue, there are a few points of interest without markers or memorials that are nonetheless worth exploring. The bunkers and trenches of **WN 60** (in a field off a track marked Révolution; /// warmers.asides.toward) are well preserved and graffiti-free, and have a perfect view along the whole beach. It's likely that WN 60 was among the first German bunkers to spot the Allied invasion fleet, and WN 60 and WN 62 lower down the beach (page 68) were the first to challenge the ships bearing down on them by firing recognition flares – there was no reply.

What is not clear is whether Major Werner Pluskat, the commander of the 1st Battalion, 352nd Artillery Regiment, at **WN 59** further east saw the fleet. In the movie *The Longest Day* (page 24) on which Pluskat was an adviser, he was woken at his digs in Étréham and went to his observation bunker. But that is disputed: the officer in command of WN 62, Oberleutnant Frerking, reportedly spent much of D-Day trying to reach Pluskat at his digs, at his bunker and at his HQ, to no avail. Pluskat's observation bunker, now hidden, was on the cliffs a few hundred metres west of the beach at **Sainte-Honorine-des-Pertes** (/// crossbow.signposts.journeying) which these days is suffering heavily from cliff erosion. At the bottom of the narrow rue de Mer, a ramp runs down on to the beach. This is the (unmarked) site where US forces brought some of their fuel supplies ashore using pipelines. From here, on 9 June, engineers started installing two floating 15cm pipes called 'tombolas', which extended 1km out to sea where they were each attached to a buoy. Medium-size tankers could plug into these pipes and offload their precious cargo. Onshore, the fuel pipeline ran inland for almost 4km to fuel tanks at Le Mont Cauvin. The system became operational on 16 June 1944 and remained so until 10 October.

The easternmost house at the side of the gully at Sainte-Honorine-des-Pertes (/// pick.transcripts.fateful) was used as the **house of the enthusiastic Frenchman** in *The Longest Day*, who watched a German soldier (played by Gert Fröbe) on his horse delivering milk to the gunners each day, and then joyfully waved his flag when the Allied ships opened fire.

South of Colleville-sur-Mer The sleepy little commune of Blay (12km from Colleville), which had been occupied by the German 916th Grenadier Regiment (352nd Infantry Division), was attacked and liberated on 9 June by the 26th Infantry Regiment (US 1st Division) as they were moving inland from Omaha Beach.

OPERATION AQUATINT

Sainte-Honorine-des-Pertes (see above) has one other, earlier, claim to fame. It was the target of a failed raid by the British Small Scale Raiding Force (62 Commando) in September 1942. The plan was for 11 men to go ashore at night from a motor torpedo boat, gather intelligence about the area and capture a German guard. It went wrong from the start: they landed on the wrong beach (near the present-day site of the American Cemetery, page 67), and were discovered within minutes. All were captured or killed and the boat stuttered home with a damaged engine. A small bronze plaque on the sea wall just west of the Omaha Beach signal monument (page 138) commemorates the commandos on Operation Aquatint (/// flapper.dignitary.lease).

GENERAL OMAR BRADLEY

Omar Nelson Bradley first came to prominence in North Africa where, as a lieutenant general, he acted as Eisenhower's front-line troubleshooter, eventually taking over II Corps from General Patton. He led II Corps in the final battles in Tunisia and then in the invasion of Sicily, building a reputation as a skilled tactician and as 'the GIs' general' for his attention to the care of his men.

On D-Day, Bradley was the commander of the US First Army, which, alongside the British Second Army, made up General Montgomery's 21st Army Group. As such, he was the ground commander for all American forces in Normandy. He may have been directly answerable to Montgomery during Operation Overlord, but he was still very much Eisenhower's man.

By the end of the war in Europe, Bradley had command of all US ground forces invading Germany from the west. At one point he commanded 1.3 million men in 43 divisions, the largest body of American soldiers ever to serve under a single field commander. After the war, he became chief of staff of the United States Army and later oversaw policy-making for the Korean War, before retiring from active service in 1953. He died in 1981.

A grey marble **memorial slab** (on the bank at the junction of D96 & D97A) records two major events: the liberation of Blay on 9 June and the arrival here of General Montgomery's tactical HQ on 23 June. Just 100m east on the D96 is another **marker for Montgomery's tactical HQ**, a grey marble lectern featuring a map, annotated only in French, that shows the layout of this HQ in the fields in front. This was Montgomery's second HQ location after his first in the grounds of the Château de Creullet (page 53). It is where Lieutenant General Omar Bradley (see above) and General George Patton (page 103) came to meet him on 7 July. Patton had just flown into Normandy the day before, so this press photo opportunity was Patton and his boss, Bradley, paying their respects to their overall commander, Montgomery. Monty clearly felt at ease in Blay: another well-known photograph shows him here with his two puppies, Hitler and Rommel, and his cage of canaries in the background.

SAINT-LAURENT-SUR-MER

As with the other villages overlooking Omaha Beach, Saint-Laurent-sur-Mer, 3km west of Colleville-sur-Mer, suffered from bombing and artillery fire on D-Day, but was not the scene of heavy ground fighting. That took place in front of the two draws (page 137) from the beach up to the village, both of which were heavily defended. Today, small holiday houses line the beach and narrow roads, bordered by thick hedges, climb the hill to the centre of the village.

WHAT TO SEE AND DO
Omaha Beach signal stone and 'Les Braves' sculpture (Av de la Libération, next to Omaha Beach car park) Here you'll find one of the original D-Day carved **signal stones** (page 138). On the beach in front of it is one of the best-known artworks on the Normandy coast, the **'Les Braves' sculpture**, depicting stainless steel wings erupting from the sand, or the waves. The three sets of 9m-high wings (in total weighing around 15 tonnes) are embedded in the sand, so the sea interacts

6

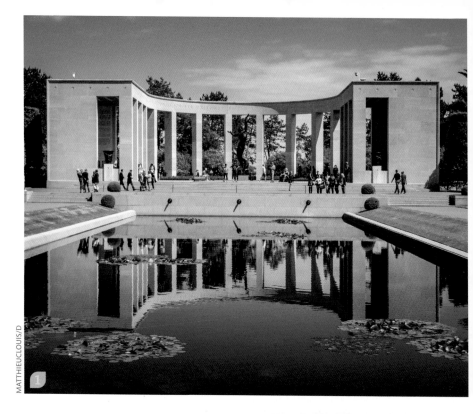

VINCENT RUSTUEL/CALVADOS ATTRACTIVITÉ

MATTHIEUCLOUIS/D

BRIGHTONGRANNY/D

WIKIMEDIA COMMONS

with them on each tide. The French artist, Anilore Banon, says they each hold a different message: the central wings represent standing up for freedom, while the ones on the sides are the wings of hope and the wings of fraternity, in honour of those who paid the ultimate sacrifice. However, even on the information panel she does not reveal which is which. Just to the west, on the beach, is the **Operation Aquatint plaque** (page 70).

Memorial Museum of Omaha Beach (Les Moulins Draw, av de la Libération; ℡ 02 31 21 97 44; w musee-memorial-omaha.com; ⊕ Feb–Oct daily, hours vary, check website; adult/child €7.50/4.50) This popular museum halfway up the Saint-Laurent Draw, focusing on the events at Omaha Beach and Pointe du Hoc, is not large, but manages to feel light and spacious while still packing in plenty of dioramas, vehicles and equipment. There are some very interesting historical photographs and documents, and a cinema showing a documentary film using veterans' testimonies.

Memorials A rough stone block marks the edge of **A-21c ALG** (unnamed road off rue Bernard Dargols; /// charms.assails.pincers) on the bluffs above Omaha Beach. The US 834th Engineer Aviation Battalion quickly carved out the runway for this advanced landing ground (page 52) on 8 June, and the first aircraft, a C-47 transport plane, landed at 06.00 on 9 June. The airstrip was a logistics hub for the 9th Air Force Service Command, but it was also designated as an emergency landing strip.

The German **WN 65** bunker (off rue Bernard Dargols; /// sandpit.subtexts. meerkat), which, remarkably, still contains its 50mm anti-tank gun, brings home the frightening reality of facing enemy fire, through the damage inflicted on it, particularly to the armour shield, by two 37mm guns on US half-track vehicles. Outside, on the wall, a plaque commemorates its use, after capture, as the HQ for the Provisional Engineer Special Brigade Group. Next to the bunker, a tall black marble stele remembers the US **2nd Infantry Division** and those who died in the assault.

Don't miss the **Charles Shay memorial park** (on a low bluff on the edge of the beach; /// psyching.polarity.threading), established in memory of the 175 Indigenous Americans who landed at Omaha on D-Day, part of the estimated 500 indigenous troops who landed in Normandy by air or sea on 6 June. Charles Shay, of the Penobscot tribe in Maine, was a US army medic in the 16th Infantry Regiment, 1st Division and was just a few weeks away from his 20th birthday when he landed in the first wave at Omaha Beach. His actions on that day, pulling wounded men from the water and tending to them immediately, earned him a US Silver Star and the French Légion d'Honneur. The park has a bust of Shay, who is now a tribal elder, and a ceremonial turtle made by his nephew, Timothy Shay. On 27 June 2024 he will be 100 years old.

VIERVILLE-SUR-MER

Vierville-sur-Mer sits at the top of the steep gully, or draw (page 137), that runs up from the western end of Omaha Beach. Of the five draws from Omaha beach, this was the only one with a paved road, making it the most obvious exit route from

◀ 1 The vast Normandy American Cemetery in Colleville-sur-Mer. 2 The 'Les Braves' sculpture in Saint-Laurent-sur-Mer. 3 A visitor gazes upon some of the items on display at the Overlord Museum. 4 Montgomery playing with his puppies, Hitler and Rommel, on 6 July 1944, at his second tactical HQ outside Blay.

The British government had turned down all women journalists who applied to cover the D-Day landings. Martha Gellhorn, a seasoned American war correspondent for *Collier's* magazine, was not deterred. On 5 June 1944, she approached a hospital ship on the south coast of England, claiming she was there to interview six nurses. She went on board and hid in a bathroom as the ship made its way across the English Channel.

Gellhorn, who was married during the war to Ernest Hemingway and was a friend of Eleanor Roosevelt, wrote in a *Collier's* article in August 1944 that, as they approached the coast of France, they passed a landing craft 'with washing hung up on a line, and between the loud explosions of mines being detonated on the beach, one could hear dance music coming from its radio'. The only female journalist to cover D-Day first-hand, her dispatches were full of details that brought the war home to her readers on the other side of the world.

Later in the war, she travelled with the US Army's 82nd Airborne Division, witnessing the Battle of the Bulge and the liberation of Dachau. Her career lasted over 60 years, covering events including the Nuremberg war trials and all the world's major conflicts. She died in 1998, aged 89, at her home in London, and remains one of the world's great war journalists.

Martha Gellhorn with Ernest Hemingway.

the beach. As a result, it was heavily fortified, turning it into a killing zone. Some of the fiercest fighting on Omaha took place here; US casualties were so heavy in front of the draw that, at 07.30, an hour after the assault started, that part of the beach was closed to further landings. Instead, they fought their way up the bluffs on either side and captured the village at 10.30, but it took until 16.30 for the massive concrete wall blocking the way off the beach to be blown up, clearing the way for vehicles.

Nowadays the draw is busy with tourists. The large car park at the bottom is in continuous churn, with coaches and cars arriving and leaving. Around it are beach shops, eateries and a hotel. The nearest **tourist information centre** is in Isigny-Omaha or in Isigny-sur-Mer (page 67).

D-Day Omaha Museum (Rte de Grandcamp/D514, near the junction with D517;
02 31 21 71 80; w dday-omaha.fr; Apr–May & Sep 10.30–18.00 daily; Jun–Aug 10.00–19.00 daily; Oct–Nov groups of 10+ only, booked in advance; adult/child 8–15 years/under-8s €7/4/free;) This small, private museum is housed in a former easy-to-build Quonset hut, a semi-cylindrical corrugated steel structure, originally used as a field hospital. Outside there's a pair of 130mm naval guns from the French destroyer *Le Chacal*, which was sunk off Boulogne-sur-Mer in May 1940, and an extraordinary, huge, armoured bell turret, originally from the Maginot Line (France's border defences, which, in May 1940, were easily surpassed by the Germans) and incorporated into the Germans' Atlantic Wall defences. Inside, the space is full of equipment, uniforms, small arms and larger guns. There's an enigma machine, a US Army field hospital tent with its equipment, and an excellent model of the beach and buildings on 6 June 1944, giving you a clear and chilling idea of what the troops were up against.

Memorials The drive down the Vierville Draw (D517) from the D-Day Omaha Museum to the beach passes several memorials and landmarks. Firstly, five sections of the huge iron **Mulberry A bridge spans**, or 'whales' (page 55), run along the west side of the road. Opposite, a stone commemorates the **6th Engineer Special Brigade** (/// dither.weekends.shakily), who cleared the western end of Omaha Beach of obstacles and then ran supplies and reinforcements ashore on landing craft and amphibious trucks after Mulberry A was destroyed, until the beach operations ceased in mid-November 1944, when the war had moved on. Further along on the east, a stone remembers the US **29th Infantry Division** (/// uses.pestle.scuttles), who formed a key part of the forces here. As the road reaches the beachfront, there are more memorials to the west: a statue of a soldier dragging a wounded comrade, dedicated to the **29th Infantry Division** (cnr of rue de la Percée); a **US National Guard** memorial on the site of the former bunker, WN 72; a light grey stone to RAF radar and radio technicians of the **2nd Tactical Air Force** (/// speculative.angling. snipped); and a memorial to the US **58th Armored Field Artillery Battalion** (/// reclaimed.healer.enraging).

POINTE DU HOC AND AROUND

The area along the coast and inland to the west of Omaha Beach has some key sites of interest. The promontory at Pointe du Hoc is one of Normandy's most visited D-Day sites, but the bizarrely named nearby town of Grandcamp-Maisy and the German cemetery at La Cambe get little attention, yet are well worth a visit.

TOURIST INFORMATION

Isigny-sur-Mer tourist information office (page 67); w isignyomaha-tourisme.fr; hours vary, but often 09.30–12.30 & 14.00–18.00; check website.

Grandcamp-Maisy tourist information office 26 quai Crampon; 02 31 21 46 00; w isigny-omaha-tourisme.fr; same hours as Isigny-sur-Mer tourist office.

Pointe du Hoc Battery and Ranger monument (D514A; 02 31 51 62 00;
w abmc.gov/Pointe-du-Hoc; main site daily, visitor centre Apr–Sep 30 09.00–18.00 daily, Oct–Mar 09.00–17.00 daily; free; guided tours) You get little sense of the scale of Pointe du Hoc as you walk to the visitor centre – but when you

Not every man assaulting Pointe du Hoc was a US Ranger. Lieutenant Colonel Thomas Trevor was a British Royal Commando who had trained the Rangers in climbing techniques on similar cliffs on the Isle of Wight. He joined them on the assault and was wounded. The Rangers also acquired three paratroopers from the 101st Airborne Division, who had been badly mis-dropped on the shoreline a few hours earlier.

get to the main viewpoint, on top of the command/observation bunker, and look down, you realise how formidable a task it was for US troops to attack. The Allies feared Pointe du Hoc, with its 155mm artillery aimed towards Utah and Omaha beaches, could cause heavy casualties, so the orders to Lieutenant Colonel James E Rudder, commander of the 2nd Ranger Battalion, were brief: land at 06.30 on D-Day on the beach below, climb the 30m-high cliffs and take out the German positions. By 07.40, most of the Rangers had reached the top, only to find the gun positions empty. The mobile 155mm howitzers had been moved from their open gun pits to make way for new casemates, which had not been completed when the rangers struck. As the fierce fighting continued, the Rangers discovered the missing howitzers unguarded a few hundred metres away, and destroyed them using thermite charges. The Rangers stayed on Pointe du Hoc under siege from German forces until the morning of 8 June, when they were relieved. Only around 90 Rangers were still standing from the original force of 225. The site today remains a blasted wasteland of huge craters, dotted with the remains of concrete bunkers and casemates, stretching back from the cliffs, and information boards with maps and images describing the action and some of the men involved. The monument to the Rangers takes the form of a 6m-tall, rough stone obelisk on top of the command bunker. If you can, book a tour with a park ranger, who will take you round the different buildings, which functioned as living quarters, gun emplacements and a hospital. In recent years the cliffs have been suffering badly from erosion. Each year another section of footpath is closed to the public, so don't put off a visit.

World Peace statue and Frank Peregory memorial stone (Rte de Vierville/ D514, by the junction with rue Gambetta, Grandcamp-Maisy) Along the coastal road, 3.5km away on the eastern edge of Grandcamp-Maisy, there is a 10m-tall stainless steel statue of a female figure in flowing dress and long sleeves. It's the work of Chinese artist Yao Yuan and was unveiled at the 60th D-Day anniversary (2004). Just in front, a US National Guard memorial stone remembers Technical Sergeant Frank D Peregory, who won the Congressional Medal of Honor, the USA's highest award, for his action on 8 June. He stormed a machine-gun post in Grandcamp-Maisy with grenades and a bayonet, killing eight and capturing 35 enemy soldiers. Sadly he was killed six days later.

Maisy Battery (7 Les Perruques, Grandcamp-Maisy; e info@maisybattery.com; w maisybattery.com; ⏱ Apr–May & Sep 10.00–17.00 daily, Jun–Aug 10.00–19.00 daily; last entry 1hr before closing; adult/child 6–18 years €8/5; & mostly; a few buildings and trenches are not, but they provide a map showing wheelchair access)

---

1 The soaring cliffs of Pointe du Hoc, topped by the German battery, were a formidable obstacle for US landing forces. 2 The tumulus holding the mass grave of 295 German soldiers at La Cambe cemetery. ▶

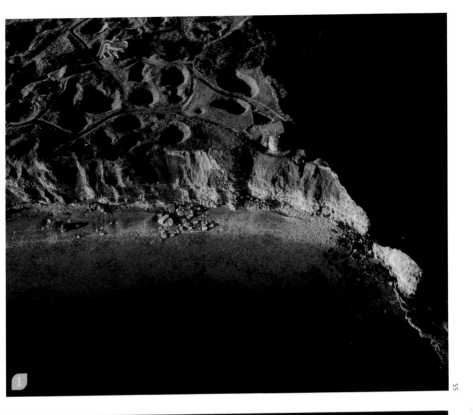

Maisy Battery is a bit mysterious. For some reason it was covered up (literally) at the end of the war, and it was only down to the diligent detective work of World War II historian and collector, Gary Sterne, that the 58ha site was re-discovered in 2004. Thanks to its location, its six artillery weapons (155mm World War I French field howitzers) could reach both Utah and Omaha beaches, which explains how shells were still arriving on Omaha Beach even after the battery at Longues-sur-Mer had been captured on 7 June and Pointe du Hoc had been shown to have no guns. The site is a maze of interconnecting trenches, bunkers and open gun pits. If they are there, ask Gary or his son, Dan, to tell you the story of how they discovered Maisy Battery.

La Cambe German military cemetery (Next to the N13/E46 dual carriageway; come off at the La Cambe junction and follow signs to the cemetery; ⏰ 08.00–19.00 daily; free; ♿) Some 8km inland near the town of La Cambe, this cemetery only covers 6.7ha but contains a remarkable 21,222 German graves. Unlike the Commonwealth cemeteries, La Cambe is a sombre place. Instead of large white stones engraved with the insignia, name, dates and a simple message on each gravestone, the German dark stone markers, in the shape of the Iron Cross German medal, are packed closely together, lying on the ground. Two soldiers are buried beneath each one, marked with just their names and sometimes birth and death dates. For unknown soldiers, where the CWGC cemeteries have 'Known unto God', the grave bears the words *'Ein Deutscher Soldat'* ('a German soldier'). Small standing crosses, in groups of five, stand at regular intervals among the graves. In the middle, a central green tumulus contains the mass grave of 295 soldiers, their markers running around the bottom. The only vegetation is the mature oak trees that dot the site. It's a sad place, with a brooding Gothic feel, made sadder by the ages of so many of them. They range from 16 to 72, but many were just 18 and they died in those few intense weeks between 6 June and 20 August 1944. Above all, the cemetery brings home the futility and waste of war – for every soldier, whatever nationality.

The cemetery was created by the United States Army Graves Registration Service in 1944, as a mixed site, with German dead buried in one field and American dead in the next. After the war, the American dead were either repatriated or reburied at the Normandy American Cemetery, and the La Cambe site was taken over by the German War Graves Commission who, in 1954, began to gather the remains of German soldiers from small graveyards and burial sites scattered around Normandy into six large cemeteries. La Cambe received an extra 12,000 dead. The small gatehouse has commemorative plaques and a modern visitor centre outside has a database of the graves.

US ALGs American engineers were busy building airstrips in this area in the days after D-Day. A rough standing stone marks the eastern end of **A-1 ALG** (off D514 between Vierville-sur-Mer & Grandcamp-Maisy; /// messily.necessary. snowy), which the 834th Engineer Aviation Battalion started building on 7 June. They completed a 1,000m runway by the evening of 8 June, when it opened as an emergency landing strip. It was used by Piper L4 artillery-spotter aircraft until it was upgraded to a full ALG, with a 1,525m runway, and the 9th US Air Force's 366th Fighter Group moved in with their P-47 Thunderbolts on 17 June – the first fighter group to move to France from England. As the war front shifted, the squadron moved to Dreux on 24 August.

Southwest, towards La Cambe, **A-2 ALG** (La Grande Lande, Cricqueville-en-Bessin; /// roams.darken.shiver) is marked with a large stone, which records that the 354th Fighter Group (P-51 Mustangs) were here from 17 June to 15 August. It doesn't record that the airfield had been built by 820th Engineer Aviation Battalion in 11 days, from 9 June, nor that the 354th were replaced by the 367th Fighter Group (P-38 Lightnings), who had previously been based at A-14 ALG on the Cotentin (page 80). Pilot Erny Snow was not impressed with the A-2's wildlife: 'Biggest nuisance is the darn bees, at chowtime a fellow has to use one hand to bat away the bees. Mess area is out in a pasture and sort of picnic type eating goes on. I got stung on the tongue and Scheffler got stung on the lower lip which swelled up and looked like a horse's lower lip.'

At **A-3 ALG** (Cardonville, southwest of A-2 ALG; /// authenticity.mission.lamps) the stone marker proudly declares that on 18 June, the USAAF 368th Fighter Group (P-47 Thunderbolts) were the first group to become operational in France. (On the face of it, it could be wrong. The 366th and 354th were operational from ALGs A-1 and A-2 a day earlier, but nearly all the records and historians disagree about ALG dates.) The marker for **A-4 ALG** (cnr of D204 & La Vallée, La Cambe) remembers the 48th Fighter Group (P-47 Thunderbolts) who were based there from 18 June to 5 September.

RAF Lancaster memorial and solitary grave (Église Saint-Clément, Osmanville)

(Église Saint-Clément, Osmanville) In the churchyard of this small village, 8km southwest of Grandcamp-Maisy, there is a black marble stone dedicated to seven airmen from RAF 97 Squadron, and a solitary CWGC grave nearby. This squadron was a Bomber Command pathfinder squadron, and the airmen named were a Lancaster crew, captained by Lieutenant Finn Varde. They were shot down near Osmanville on the night of 5–6 June 1944, on a mission to bomb the gun battery at Pointe du Hoc before the landings. Lieutenant Jespersen and five other crew members were from the Norwegian Air Force and their bodies were repatriated to Norway. A sixth crew member, Pilot Officer Robert McCutcheon from the Royal Canadian Air Force, was taken to Bayeux CWGC cemetery. That left the flight engineer, 18-year-old Sergeant G J J Ashpole from Gravesend in Kent, who is buried in the lone CWGC grave.

6

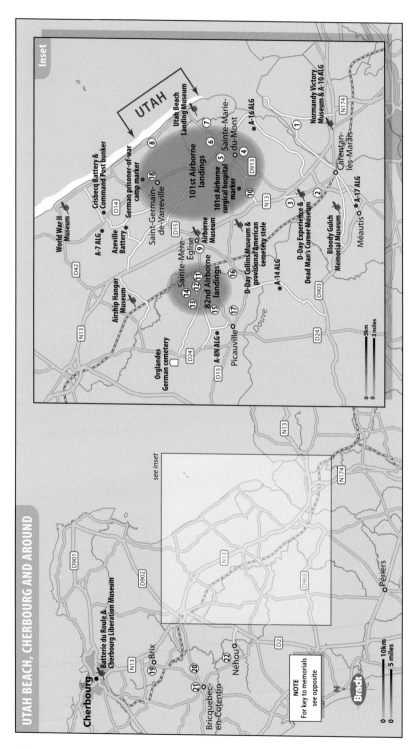

Inset

UTAH

Utah Beach
Landing Museum ⑦

Sainte-Marie-
du-Mont

A-16 ALG ①

Normandy Victory
Museum & A-10 ALG

N174

Carentan-
les-Marais

Crisbecq Battery &
Command Post bunker

German prisoner-of-war
camp marker ⑱

⑥ Saint-Marie-
du-Mont

①

World War II
Museum

A-7 ALG ●

D14

Saint-Germain-
de-Varreville

101st Airborne
landings

⑤ 101st Airborne
surgical hospital
marker

④ D913

⑩

N13

② A-17 ALG

Azeville
Battery

D15

⑨ Airborne
Museum

③

D-Day Experience &
Dead Man's Corner Museum

Méautis ●

Airship Hangar
Museum

Sainte-Mère-
Église

⑬ ⑭

⑫ ⑪

82nd Airborne
landings

⑮

⑯

D-Day Collins Museum &
provisional American
cemetery stele

A-14 ALG ●

Bloody Gulch
Memorial Museum

D903

N13

Orglandes
German cemetery

D24

D15 A-8N ALG ●

Picauville ○

⑰

Douve

D24

0   5km
0   3 miles

see inset

N13

N174

D903

N13

Cherbourg ●

Batterie du Roule &
Cherbourg Liberation Museum

D901

N13 ○ Brix

D902

⑲ ○ ⑳

㉒ ○ Néhou

D902

Bricquebec-
en-Cotentin

㉑

D2

Périers ○

NOTE
For key to memorials
see opposite

0   10km
0   5 miles

Bradt

80

7

Utah Beach, Cherbourg and Around

Utah Beach was an afterthought. At the start of 1944, generals Dwight Eisenhower (page 82) and Bernard Montgomery (page 26) realised that the existing plan for the invasion was simply too thin. They needed to double the size of the landing areas and their forces, and since securing the deep-water port of Cherbourg was of primary importance, landing troops on the Cotentin Peninsula would also speed up that objective.

Utah Beach came perilously close to being prematurely revealed as an invasion target. One convoy of landing craft that had set off from South Devon on 4 June did not hear the recall message when D-Day was postponed by 24 hours. A flying boat was quickly dispatched in a desperate search for them, and eventually found them just 58km from Normandy. It dropped coded messages in canisters, and the convoy turned back.

While Allied intelligence may have underestimated German defences at Omaha, it over estimated their strength on Utah. In addition, a strong tide deposited the first wave of troops 1.8km to the south, where there was only one defence strongpoint instead of the two they were expecting.

Utah Beach turned out to be the least troublesome of the D-Day beaches. Some 21,000 US troops came ashore on Utah, with only 197 casualties. The airborne divisions further inland fared worse, suffering 2,500 casualties from a force of 14,000 men. Scattered all over their landing zones, many found themselves isolated and fighting small group actions against hardened German paratroopers. In addition, the Germans had deliberately flooded large areas and many US paratroopers were impeded or drowned in the waters. Despite their problems, they persevered, and once the ground forces were ashore the Americans

UTAH BEACH, CHERBOURG AND AROUND

○ **Memorials**

1 Filthy Thirteen (US) *p85*
2 Cole's Bayonet Charge (US) *p86*
3 Lt Col Robert Lee Wolverton (US) *p87*
4 Normandy French Resistance statue *p89*
5 Easy Company (US) *p89*
6 Major Richard D Winters (US) *p89*
7 Danish Sailors *p90*
8 8th Infantry Division (US) & 2nd Armoured Division (FR) *p90*
9 505th PIR & Theodore Roosevelt Jr (US) *p91*
10 Brig Gen Don Pratt (US) *p92*
11 La Fière memorial park & Iron Mike (US) *p93*
12 325th GIR & Charles DeGlopper (US) *p93*
13 507th PIR & Joe Gandara (US) *p94*
14 Lt Col Charles J Timmes (US) *p94*
15 Captain Maternowski (US) *p94*
16 508th PIR memorial & garden (US) *p96*
17 C-47 plaques & garden (US) *p96*
18 101st Airborne Division (US) *p99*
19 USAAF B-17 and P-47 (US) *p102*
20 B-17 (US) *p102*
21 Pyramid of Memory *p102*
22 Camp Patton memorial park *p103*

Utah Beach, Cherbourg and Around

7

81

Supreme Allied Commander Dwight D Eisenhower was an extraordinary wartime leader. He was a good military strategist and a decisive commander, but his real skill was diplomacy. Keeping together a coalition of Allied generals, admirals, air marshals and politicians with different national interests and characteristics, and keeping them working together and 'on mission', required superhuman skill – and that is what Eisenhower provided.

General Eisenhower addressing paratroopers on 5 June 1944.

Eisenhower was a career soldier who was commissioned as a second lieutenant in the US Army in 1915, although he was never sent to the front line. In 1941 he was appointed commander of the US 9th Infantry Division, before being promoted in 1943 to Supreme Commander of the Allied Expeditionary Force, which was responsible for planning and executing the invasion of Normandy. It was Eisenhower who took the decision to launch the Normandy invasion in a short gap in the otherwise bad weather. Luck and good judgement were with him, and D-Day was a success. Eisenhower then led the Allied forces in a series of campaigns that eventually led to the liberation of France and the defeat of Nazi Germany.

After the war, he served as the first supreme commander of NATO, and he played a key role in the development of the Marshall Plan, which helped to rebuild Europe. Eisenhower retired from the military in 1952, and served two terms as US president from the following year. He died in 1969 at the age of 78.

were able to meet their objectives – the Cotentin Peninsula was cut off by 18 June and Cherbourg captured by 27 June.

The Cotentin is rich in D-Day sites. From the museums in and around Carentan-les-Marais, Sainte-Mère-Église and Utah Beach itself, to the numerous memorials scattered about the key airborne battlegrounds, and the bunkers and batteries of the Atlantic Wall, there is plenty to see and explore. The Cotentin Peninsula could take up a whole Normandy trip by itself.

GETTING THERE AND AROUND

The Cotentin covers a wide area, with two main entry points: Cherbourg in the north and Carentan-les-Marais in the south. But public transport is sparse, so **driving** is the best way to get around. You can get from Cherbourg to Carentan by **train** (28mins); if you are arriving at the **ferry** terminal, you have to get to Cherbourg train station (2.4km). From Carentan, local **buses** go to some key places like Sainte-Mère-Église (see individual towns for more information). But to see many of the sites you will need to drive or take a **tour**.

CARENTAN-LES-MARAIS AND AROUND

Carentan-les-Marais, with its marina and its 15th-century church (restored after World War II bombing), is an attractive, small, rural town. On the edge of the Douve

River and with its extensive marshlands, it was strategically important to both the Allies and the Germans. In the first few days after D-Day, the Allied objective was to link all the beachheads into one front, but stubborn German resistance meant that US forces were not expanding from their bridgeheads as quickly as General Eisenhower would have liked. Germany's Field Marshal Erwin Rommel, too, saw that German-occupied Carentan, sitting in the gap between Omaha and Utah beaches, was an opportunity to drive a wedge between the US forces, and he ordered the 17th SS Panzergrenadier Division into the area. At the same time, the US 101st Airborne Division was given orders to capture it. The battle lines were set.

In the ensuing battle, the 101st Airborne Division fought their way south from the Cotentin, across the causeway over the marshes, and across the River Taute into Carentan on 10 June. The fighting became bloody and hand-to-hand. In the late afternoon on 11 June, the American and German paratroopers agreed a brief ceasefire so they could collect their dead and wounded, after which fighting resumed. On 12 June the Germans had exhausted their ammunition and pulled out of Carentan. The next day the German 17th SS Panzergrenadier Division mounted a heavy assault on Carentan, which the Americans managed to hold off while they waited for armoured support. On 14 June Carentan was secured. Since this had been, for the most part, a paratrooper-on-paratrooper battle with light arms, the town was relatively unscathed.

There's a **tourist information office** near the war memorial in the centre (24 pl de la République; ℡02 33 71 23 50; w ot-baieducotentin.fr; ⊕ Apr–Jun & Sep 09.30–12.30 & 14.00–18.00 Mon–Sat, 09.30–13.30 bank hols except 1 May; Jul–Aug 09.00–18.30 Mon–Sat, 10.00–16.00 Sun & bank hols; Oct–Mar 09.30–12.30 & 14.00–18.00 Mon–Fri, closed bank hols).

GETTING THERE AND AROUND By **car**, Carentan-les-Marais sits on the main N13 route between Cherbourg (52.2km; 48mins) and Ouistreham (86.8km; 1hr). You can also get to Carentan by **train** from Cherbourg (approx 12/day; 28mins) and from Caen (approx 14/day; 41mins). By **bus**, take the 301 from Cherbourg (around 6/day; 1hr 10mins); there's no direct bus from Caen. A good bus service in Carentan takes you around town and to nearby beaches (Cap Cotentin; w capcotentin.fr/lignes-regulieres; single €1 if bought in advance at the tourist information office or a tabac, €1.50 on board, €4 for an all-day ticket). Carentan is a pretty town, and it's easy to **walk** and **cycle** around.

WHAT TO SEE AND DO
East of Carentan
Normandy Victory Museum (Musée de la Bataille des Haies; rue de la Fourchette; ℡02 33 71 74 94; w normandy-victory-museum.fr; ⊕ Feb–Dec, hours & days vary, check website; adult/child €9/6; ♿) This museum was opened in 2016 by three enthusiastic local historians and collectors, and is bigger than you expect from the outside. Most of its 15,000 artefacts are presented in 27 highly detailed and realistic dioramas in 15,000m² of display space. The museum focuses on the experiences of civilians and soldiers during the 100 days following D-Day, and particularly during the Battle of the Hedges as the Allies fought their way through the bocage (page 106). However, it's not just scenes of soldiers in Normandy fields and villages – look out for the recreation of a French POW camp in Germany, and the gallery on the role of women in the armed forces. The museum has an easy feel to it: they encourage photography; they welcome pets and motorhomes; it's fully accessible (all on one floor). Their retro-style brasserie/pizzeria at the front

7

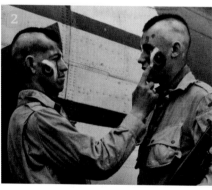

is always full of families stopping for lunch or snacks. The museum was built on the site of the **A-10 advanced landing ground** (page 52), and it offers a 40-minute tour around the ALG from outside the museum entrance in a Dodge WC51 vintage military vehicle, with an English-speaking guide. It also offers a 75-minute tour into the town of Carentan and the bocage. Meanwhile a small grey monument (1.8km from the museum via D974 & D89; /// daylight.zoos.revalue) marks the eastern end of the ALG's runway. A-10 was constructed between 14 and 16 June by the US 826th Engineer Aviation Battalion, and was the base for squadrons from the 9th USAAF 50th Fighter Group flying P-47 Thunderbolts, and the 367th Fighter Group (392nd Fighter Squadron) in P-38 Lightnings. The base remained operational until 4 November.

Filthy Thirteen memorial (Rue du Moulin/D89E, 200m north of the junction with rue Phosphates, 4.2km northeast of Carentan centre; /// assurances.brushwork. toner) Troops of the 'Filthy Thirteen' demolition platoon, from the 506th Parachute Infantry Regiment (PIR) of the US 101st Airborne Division, were famous for their unruly behaviour, disrespect for officers, hard drinking and savage fighting skills – although, unlike in the movie they inspired, *The Dirty Dozen*, they were not ex-convicts. They were photographed on 5 June, just before boarding their aircraft to go to Normandy, with heads shaved in a Mohican style and warpaint on their faces.

Although the memorial is generally called the 'Filthy Thirteen', it honours the whole of the 3rd Battalion of the 506th PIR, to whom they were attached. The battalion's mission was to capture or destroy two nearby bridges over the Carentan canal to prevent the Germans using them to attack the Utah beachhead – very similar to the Pegasus Bridge operation at Sword Beach (page 20). Of the 575 men who jumped, 93 were killed, including commanding officer Lieutenant Colonel Robert Lee Wolverton (page 87), and 75 were captured. The bridges were reached, but were too heavily defended to capture, and in the end were destroyed by US aircraft. A small garden features a statue of Filthy Thirteen sergeant Jake McNiece, kneeling in front of a stone plinth that explains the mission. There is a remembrance tree and a smaller stone pedestal with a carved eagle dedicated simply to the US Airborne forces.

West of Carentan

D-Day Experience and Dead Man's Corner Museum (2 village de l'Amont, Saint-Côme-du-Mont; ☏ 02 33 23 61 95; w dday-experience.com; ◷ Apr–Sep 09.30–19.00 daily; Oct–Mar 10.00–18.00 daily; adult/child €13.90/10.90) One of Normandy's newest D-Day sites, the D-Day Experience, has been added to one of its oldest, the Dead Man's Corner Museum, with the site now comprising museum exhibits, an immersive airborne experience, 3D cinema and a wall of remembrance to US paratroopers.

At the northern end of the single causeway that runs across the marshlands of the Douve River, the road splits either side of a two-storey stone house, making it a strategically important chokepoint in June 1944. For that reason, on D-Day, Major Friedrich von der Heydte, commanding the German 6th Parachute Regiment, set up his HQ here and quickly came under attack by American paratroopers of

7

◀ 1 The Dead Man's Corner Museum in Saint-Côme-du-Mont is one of the oldest in Normandy. 2 & 3 The notorious 'Filthy Thirteen' demolition platoon, who wore warpaint and had Mohican-style haircuts, are honoured with a statue near Carentan. 4 The Normandy Victory Museum has highly detailed, realistic dioramas.

Taken from King Henry's rallying speech to his troops on the eve of the Battle of Agincourt in Shakespeare's play *Henry V*, *Band of Brothers* was the title author Stephen E Ambrose chose for his 1992 book following the real-life story of Easy Company from the 2nd Battalion, 506th Parachute Infantry Regiment of the 101st Airborne Division. When Tom Hanks and Steven Spielberg turned the book into a hugely popular ten-part TV miniseries, Easy Company's World War II exploits in Europe, from Normandy to Berchtesgaden, became famous, as did their commander Major Richard 'Dick' Winters.

the 101st Airborne Division, including Easy Company 506th PIR – the 'Band of Brothers'. The fighting was fierce, and on the third day, the Germans withdrew to Carentan-les-Marais, leaving the house at this location, nicknamed Dead Man's Corner, to the Americans.

The house is now Dead Man's Corner Museum and has been restored to how it was as von der Heydte's HQ, with models of German paratroopers and equipment squeezed into its rooms. Behind it stands the large modern buildings of the D-Day Experience and cinema, which offers the US airborne perspective. Visitors are briefed on the mission ahead before boarding a simulated C-47 plane. TV screens in the windows show exterior views as it 'flies', gets hit by anti-aircraft (AA) fire and crash-lands in Normandy. The museum itself has some spectacular dioramas and significant artefacts, such as the battle jackets of Lieutenant Colonel Benjamin Vandervoort (who is portrayed by John Wayne in *The Longest Day*, page 24) and Dick Winters (*Band of Brothers*; see above). The cinema shows a 36-minute remastered version of Pascal Vuong's documentary *D-Day: Normandy 1944*, and a new short film covering the Battle of Carentan (3D glasses and earphones for the English audio are provided).

Bloody Gulch Memorial Museum (Manoir de Donville, Méautis; ✆ 02 33 42 03 22; w museebloodygulch.com; ⏰ May–Oct 10.00–18.00 daily, Nov–Apr 10.00–18.00 Fri–Sun; adult/child €12.50/7; reservations necessary; guided tours available with the owner) The Battle of Bloody Gulch was the German counter-attack on Carentan launched on 13 June, which met the 101st Airborne as it expanded out from the town. Easy Company 506th PIR were in the thick of it, as shown in *Band of Brothers* (episode 3). It was a hard-fought battle, which the lightly equipped American paratroopers seemed to be losing until the 29th US Infantry Division turned up with some 60 tanks from the 2nd Armoured Division.

Memorials When US 101st Airborne were tasked with taking Carentan on 10 June, Lieutenant Colonel Robert G Cole of the 3rd Battalion, 502nd PIR led 400 men, facing continuous German fire, along the 1.5km causeway that runs across the Douve River floodplain. Reaching the end, they met fierce resistance from German paratroopers dug in around a farm building. A heavy artillery attack the following day failed to dislodge them, so Cole called for a smoke barrage to cover a bayonet charge on the building. The attack was costly but successful and Cole was awarded the Medal of Honor, although he was killed by a sniper on 18 September, before he could receive his medal. The **Cole's Bayonet Charge memorial** (west side of D971/D974 roundabout; /// elector.gazed.taxable) – a tall black-stone pillar with an etched image of Cole and his men charging, together with a white parachute sculpture – was erected on the 70th Anniversary of D-Day (2014).

The exposed causeway, where many soldiers were killed or wounded, including 67% of the 3rd Battalion of the 502nd PIR, became known as 'Purple Heart Lane'. On the opposite side of the D974 exit (/// slowing.mitigates.sliding) a **Purple Heart Lane** sign was erected in 2023. **Igouf Farm**, the building that had caused Cole and his men so much trouble, is 250m southwest on the D971 (/// mongrel.refers.lazy), with a small commemoration plaque inside the farm fence.

Fellow PIR leader **Lieutenant Colonel Robert Lee Wolverton**, of the 3rd Battalion, 506th PIR, is honoured 3.5km away (side road east of rue Maréchal Leclerc, just north of the junction with rte de Houesville; /// implicit.consults. motivator). Sadly, he never reached French soil: he was killed while helplessly dangling in his parachute from an apple tree close to this spot. The black granite tablet, unveiled in 2014, also pays tribute to Colonel Frank X Krebs, of the 440th Troop Carrier Group, and his pilots, who dropped Wolverton and his men on D-Day, losing three C-47 aircraft in the process.

Near the village of Méautis, 6km southwest of Carentan, a sandstone stele marks the site of **A-17 ALG** (D443, 500m north of the centre; /// calm.giant.linguistics),

LEADING FROM THE FRONT

Theodore Roosevelt Jr led a full life as both a distinguished soldier and a politician and businessman. He was the eldest son of President Theodore Roosevelt and first cousin of President Franklin D Roosevelt. He fought in World War I as a major in the US 1st Division, and, in the interwar years, served first as assistant secretary of the Navy, then governor of Puerto Rico and later governor-general of the Philippines. He also served as chairman of the board of American Express and vice president of Doubleday Books.

In 1944, Roosevelt was deputy commander of the 4th Infantry Division. Despite opposition from his commander, he insisted on going ashore with the troops, which made him the only general on D-Day to land by sea with the first wave of troops, and, at 56, the oldest man in the invasion. When he got ashore, he discovered that the tidal currents had carried them south of their target landing spot. Armed with only his walking stick (he had a heart condition and arthritis) and a pistol, he surveyed the exit routes and causeways from the beach, rallied his men, and ordered them to 'start the war from here'. His personal gallantry and decisive leadership on D-Day won him a promotion and the Medal of Honor, which had to be awarded posthumously because, on 12 July, he had a heart attack and died in the village of Méautis. That same day, Eisenhower had approved his promotion to Major General, with command of the US 90th Division. He is buried in the Normandy American Cemetery (page 67).

This statue of Roosevelt was unveiled in Sainte-Mère-Église in 2023.

ALASTAIR MCKENZIE

7

where the 50th Fighter Group (P-47 Thunderbolts) of the 9th US Air Force were based from 17 August to 6 September 1944. Behind you, as you look at the monument, the first three wind turbines follow the line of the runway, which was laid by the 840th Engineer Aviation Battalion between 24 July and 16 August (the wording on the stone is not accurate).

In the village itself, by the church entrance, there is a plaque on a World War II obelisk to **Brigadier General Theodore Roosevelt Jr** (page 87), and there's another plaque on the school wall nearby, close to the place where Roosevelt died while sleeping in his truck.

SAINTE-MARIE-DU-MONT AND AROUND

The small town of Sainte-Marie-du-Mont is 6km inland from Utah Beach and 9.2km from Sainte-Mère-Église. It stands out in the surrounding countryside thanks to the extraordinary Moorish-looking domed bell tower of its Notre-Dame church, which starts out square and Gothic and ends up octagonal and Renaissance.

Sainte-Marie-du-Mont was strategically important as the first village of any size inland from Utah Beach, although there was little of tactical importance there. Around 60 German soldiers from the nearby Holdy Battery were billeted there. The village was captured with little trouble by the early afternoon on 6 June.

The Holdy Battery, however, with its four 105mm field howitzers located a kilometre west of the village, was the scene of some unpleasant fighting. One planeload of paratroopers from the 502nd PIR was dropped over the battery in the early hours of D-Day. They were killed or taken prisoner and tortured by the garrison. At dawn, when a company from the 506th PIR, aided by a dozen paratroopers of the 502nd PIR who had landed nearby, stormed the battery, they found the mutilated bodies of their comrades.

You will need a **car** to get to Sainte-Marie-du-Mont; but **walking** around the small town is easy, and surrounding sites are not far, so **cycling** is an option.

WHAT TO SEE AND DO
Utah Beach Landing Museum (Musée du Débarquement; La Madeleine; \02 33 71 53 35; w obr-beach.com; ⏲ May–Sep 09.30–19.00 daily, Oct–Jan & Apr 10.00–18.00 daily (with some closures in Dec; check website), Feb–Mar 10.00–17.00 daily; last ticket 1hr before closing; adult/child €8.50/5) This is one of the key D-Day museums in Normandy. It was built right on the dunes on the location of the German Widerstandsnest 5 strongpoint, where Brigadier General Theodore Roosevelt Jnr made his famous decision to 'start the war from here' (page 87). You can't miss the Douglas B-26 Marauder twin-engined bomber inside a huge glass hanger. Although 5,157 were built, this is one of only six left in the world (the other five are in the USA). It's painted in the colours of one of the bombers that led the attack at this location on the morning of D-Day, just before the troops landed. The museum also features a landing craft vehicle personnel (LCVP) assault craft – known as a 'Higgins boat' after its designer Andrew Jackson Higgins – the only known original LCVP left from D-Day. Nearby is an LV-2 tracked 'water buffalo' landing craft, which carried up to 20 men over the beach and dunes and through the flooded marshes behind. A circular glass gallery built over the dunes includes a German tobruk with a gun turret in its original position, beach defences and trenches, and an American DUKW amphibious truck (page 138). At the end of the gallery there's a display cabinet containing personal items from Major Dick Winters and his attack on the gun battery at nearby **Brécourt Manor**, in which

he and his men efficiently silenced four 105mm guns firing on the beach. The assault, which is still taught at Westpoint Military Academy as a textbook assault, features in episode 2 of the *Band of Brothers* TV miniseries (page 86). Other items to keep an eye out for are Theodore Roosevelt Jnr's walking cane (page 87) and the wall map that General 'Lightning' Joe Collins (page 92) used to plan his assault on Cherbourg.

A number of impressive memorials stand immediately outside the museum. As a **monument to the role of LCVP craft**, there's a metal, life-size Higgins boat with three soldiers storming ashore from it, and a statue of Higgins himself to one side. Behind it, the 2.3m-tall **statue of the Lone Sailor**, a larger-than-life-size sailor with a duffel bag, is an 'everyman' figure, representing the men and women, past and present, of the US Navy. This statue, made of high-density resin bonded with bronze, is moulded from a cast sculpted by American artist Stanley Bleifeld and is one of 15 copies around the world (the original is at the United States Navy memorial in Washington DC).

Follow the path north up on to the dunes for the impressive, 3.6m-high **memorial to US Navy sailors** who participated in D-Day. The chest-height black marble plinth, pentagon-shaped to represent the five landing beaches and inscribed with the names of the ships and units involved, is the base for a statue of three symbolic figures, melded together: an officer, who stands for the leadership, planning and intelligence needed for D-Day; a sailor carrying a large shell to load a gun for shore bombardment; and a sailor on his knees to represent the naval combat demolition units and those sailors who fought ashore. Next to it, a simple grey headstone is dedicated to the **US Naval Combat Demolition units**, who were first ashore at Utah. Out of a dozen 15-man demolition units on Utah, six men were killed and 11 wounded clearing a path for the 4th Infantry Division. Further along the path large standing stones commemorate the **1st Engineer Special Brigade**, who were in charge of Utah Beach operations until 23 October. Down the steps towards the car park are the 'heroic dead' of the **90th Infantry Division**; and the **Utah Beach American Memorial**, a 6.5m-tall column of square red-granite blocks.

The Normandy French Resistance statue (Opposite 22 rue de la 101E Airborne/D913) The only D-Day site in the town of Saint-Marie-du-Mont itself, a statue of three life-size civilian characters gathered around a table, unveiled in 2021, represents the three components of the French Resistance: a man, holding a Sten gun, is a guerilla; a young woman is operating a radio in a suitcase, to represent the auxiliary; and a young boy with a bicycle depicts the underground. A circular wall surrounds the statue, on top of which 93 grey stones, in the shape of flattened parachutes, symbolise the 93 teams of British, American and French operatives who covertly parachuted into occupied France, to assist the D-Day landings through sabotage and by leading local Resistance forces against the Germans.

Memorials around Sainte-Marie-du-Mont North of the town, **Easy Company memorial** (Junction of D14 & Brécourt), a three-panel stone wall, commemorates this company of the 506th PIR (page 81). It lists the names and serial numbers of the 25 men of the regiment who did not survive D-Day and stands by the field that was the scene of their famous attack on the German battery at Brécourt Manor (see opposite). Around the corner is a larger-than-life-size bronze statue of company commander **Major Richard D Winters** (in a layby on D913, just north of the junction of D913 & D14; /// negotiates.relight.barrels; page 81). The statue – dedicated 'to all those who led their way on D-Day' and unveiled

On 1 August 1944, Free French General Philippe Leclerc and his 2nd Armoured Division came ashore at Utah Beach, the first French forces to return to their homeland. All along the route inland taken by his 16,000 men and 4,000 vehicles, in some of the villages and towns they liberated, a marker of the 'Oath of Koufra' has been installed. These markers commemorate the fulfilment of the oath taken on 2 March 1941 at the oasis of Koufra, in Libya: 'We swear to lay down our arms only on the day when our colours, our beautiful colours, will fly over the cathedral of Strasbourg'. This promise was kept when Spahi Lebrun of the 1st Moroccan Spahi Regiment unfurled the French colours at the top of Strasbourg Cathedral on 23 November 1944. (Spahis were light cavalry regiments of the French army recruited primarily from the Arab and Berber populations of Algeria, Tunisia and Morocco. Spahi comes from the Persian word 'sipahi', meaning 'horseman'). The project was set up in 2004 and more than 280 municipalities along the 2nd Armoured Division route from Utah Beach to Strasbourg have applied to the Leclerc Foundation to place a marker. More than 100 have been placed so far.

on 6 June 2012, a year after Winters' death – shows him with his rifle, crouched and moving forward, and has panoramic views down to Utah Beach.

Further north along the D913 towards Utah Beach is the **Danish sailors monument** (/// totals.responsibly.waged), a large bronze statue of a merchant seaman in a duffel coat, with binoculars hanging round his neck. It is 'in memory of the 800 Danish seamen who participated in the Normandy Landings'. When Denmark was invaded by the Germans in April 1940, thousands of Danish sailors were cut off from their homeland. Most headed for Allied ports and many enlisted with the Allied naval and merchant marine, with more than 30 Danish ships involved in the invasion of Normandy.

At the unused northern end of Utah Beach, the first to land near the German strongpoint WN 10 was the **US 8th Infantry Division** – but that was not until 4 July. A rough stone monument with a black marble plaque recalls their landing (on the dunes off D421, near the car park; /// needlessly.luminous.reshaping). A large **signal stone** (/// fattens.weathering.clinician; page 138) also honours the landing, while marking another historically significant moment: on 1 August 1944, the **French 2nd Armoured Division** came ashore here – the first Free French unit to land in France. The site here has become, quite rightly, something of a shrine to this event. Numerous stones, information panels and some of the division's vehicles, including an M3 half-track, an M4 Sherman tank and an M8 light armoured car, stand on either side of the path through the dunes. There is also the first of the 'Oath of Koufra' liberation trail markers (see above).

South of Sainte-Marie-du-Mont, **A-16 ALG**, built by the 843rd Engineer Aviation Battalion between 5 and 27 August, was the base for the 36th Fighter Group of the 9th USAAF, flying P-47 Thunderbolts; they are honoured with a waist-height red-sandstone marker (D424E1; /// restructure.satisfactory.festoons).

SAINTE-MÈRE-ÉGLISE AND AROUND

This town was a key target for US paratroopers on D-Day, and is still a key target for tourists today, being pretty much dedicated to the battlefield tour industry. The town centre is an open square dominated by the church itself, with a permanent reminder of paratrooper John Steele, in the form of a mannequin dangling from a parachute, caught up on the church tower.

In the early hours of 6 June, most of the 505th PIR landed in and around their drop zone on the western outskirts of Sainte-Mère-Église. However, two aircraft misdropped their 30 paratroopers from F Company into the town itself. Unfortunately, an incendiary bomb from an earlier raid had set a villa on fire (where the Airborne Museum is now), and instead of being asleep, the locals were all gathered in the town square, with around 50 German soldiers from the local garrison, passing water buckets to the fire brigade. At that moment, 20 paratroopers landed in the square itself and Steele's parachute got caught on the church tower. Dangling helplessly, he tried to play dead, but after 2 hours he was captured by the Germans. Twelve of his comrades died. (He actually got caught on the west side of the tower, to the left of the clock, but the mannequin is hung on the south side because it is more visible. And he wasn't alone: paratrooper Kenneth Russell got caught on a gargoyle on the roof of the nave below him, but managed to cut himself free.)

The fighting in and around Sainte-Mère-Église carried on until noon on 7 June, when ground forces from Utah Beach arrived. John Steele escaped his captors and returned to his unit, and survived the war.

Sainte-Mère-Église sits just off the N13 – if **driving**, take the exit at Neuville-au-Plain on to the D974 (from Cherbourg: 37km, 30mins; from Caen: 86km, 1hr). By **bus** from Carentan station, take the 301 (approx 18mins). Sainte-Mère-Église is compact, so easy to walk or cycle around.

There is a **tourist information office** (6 rue Eisenhower; ✆ 02 33 21 00 33; w ot-baieducotentin.fr; ⊕ Apr–Jun & Sep 09.00–13.00 & 14.00–18.00 Mon–Sat, 09.30–13.30 Sun & bank hols; Jul–Aug 09.00–18.30 Mon–Sat, 10.00–16.00 Sun and bank hols; Oct–Mar 09.30–12.30 & 13.30–17.00 Mon–Fri, 10.00–13.00 & 14.00–17.00 Sat in school hols only, closed bank hols).

WHAT TO SEE AND DO
Airborne Museum (14 rue Eisenhower; ✆ 02 33 41 41 35; w airborne-museum. org; ⊕ May–Aug 09.00–19.00 daily, Apr & Sep 09.30–18.30 daily, Oct–Mar 10.00–18.00 daily; last tickets 1hr before closing; adult/child €9/6) The Airborne Museum is dedicated to the American paratroopers of the 82nd and 101st Airborne divisions who landed in the Cotentin Peninsula in the early hours of D-Day. It's one of the most popular museums in Normandy, with over 200,000 visitors a year, and celebrates its 60th anniversary in 2024.

To mark the event, a major new building dedicated to World War II gliders is set to open in June and will include, among others, the museum's authentic CG4A WACO glider; this wasn't involved in the Normandy landings but was used for crossing the Rhine in 1945.

There will also be a new exhibition on Sainte-Mère-Église under the Occupation, covering the lives of the town's inhabitants as they faced requisitions, rationing, control of movement, compulsory work, curfews and resistance.

The museum also features a C-47 transport aircraft, with displays of paratroopers and their equipment, and a walkthrough 'experience' of dropping into Normandy at night, with detailed dioramas of what US paratroopers encountered.

Memorials in the centre A small stone pedestal (junction of D974 with the access road to the N13; /// haunts.suppress.ranches) recognises the role the **505th PIR Combat Team** had in taking Sainte-Mère-Église, the first town to be liberated in France. The team, which comprised 505th PIR, 456th Parachute Field Artillery, B Company of the 307th Airborne Engineers and 80th Airborne Anti-Aircraft Battalion, was led by General J M Gavin, who is named on a sign behind the memorial; a much-decorated hero during the war, he was nicknamed 'the jumping general', or more familiarly 'Jumpin' Jim', after his practice of actually jumping with his troops, something no other general did.

A larger-than-life-size bronze statue (at the roundabout between rue du Dr Masselin & rue de la Liberté), by sculptor Pablo Eduardo and unveiled on 5 June 2023, shows **Brigadier General Theodore Roosevelt Jr** with his walking cane (page 87).

South of Sainte-Mère-Église

Hiesville The 101st Airborne's Assistant Divisional Commander, **Brigadier General Don Pratt**, elected to go with his men in the first wave of glider reinforcements to land at Hiesville, 5.5km southeast of Sainte-Mère-Église. Pratt was sitting in the co-pilot's seat of the lead glider when it overshot the landing ground and ploughed into a hedgerow, killing him instantly. He was the first general, Allied or German, to be killed on D-Day. Two grey stone blocks are placed at a road junction, 250m from where he died (junction of rte de la Haute Follie/ D129 & rte de Rabey/D329; /// perpetually.easygoing.quiet).

Just north of the village, a tall stele marks the location of **101st Airborne surgical hospital** (rte des Goueys; /// llama.foams.negates), the first divisional surgical hospital on French soil, at the Château de Colombière. Unless you have a 4x4, it's best to approach from Hiesville. The alternative is a rough farm track.

D-Day Collins Museum (Château de Franquetot, 38 rue d'Eturville; ☎02 33 20 88 36; ⓕ; ⏰ high season 09.00–18.00 daily, low season 10.00–17.00 daily; adult/child €9/6) Château de Franquetot, 5km south of Sainte-Mère-Église, was the headquarters in July 1944 of General Joe Lawton Collins, commander of US Army VII Corps. It is unusual in that the wing of the castle that 'Lightning Joe' Collins (see below) occupied was left untouched after the Americans departed a few weeks later. Collins's office, where he, Eisenhower and Lieutenant General Omar Bradley (page 71) planned Operation Cobra (the breakout from Normandy; page 114), has been cleaned up and restored to how it was at the time, with the original wallpaper, paintings and furniture. Other rooms too are authentic recreations, and the museum, opened in

'LIGHTNING JOE'

Born in New Orleans in 1896, Joseph Lawton Collins joined the US Army in 1917. During World War I he gained a reputation for swift and decisive action, which earned him the nickname 'Lightning Joe'. When World War II broke out, Collins was appointed commander of the 25th Infantry Division. His leadership was instrumental in several key victories during the Pacific War, including the capture of Guadalcanal and New Georgia. In 1944, Collins was promoted to Major General and given command of VII Corps, a unit of the US Army in Europe. Under his bold and decisive leadership, VII Corps were able to capture Cherbourg, despite fierce resistance, on 26 June 1944 – just 20 days into the Overlord campaign. He went on to play an important role in the Allied advance through France and Germany. After the war, Collins continued to serve in the US Army until his retirement in 1954. He died in 1987 at the age of 91.

2023, also features facially accurate mannequins of key characters. The museum's owner is a collector and dealer in historic military vehicles and equipment, and the courtyard of the château usually has World War II military vehicles parked there. There is a plan to install a statue of Collins, Bradley and Eisenhower, recreating a famous photo of the three on the exact spot in the courtyard.

Just 700m north of the château, by the D70, is a stele commemorating the location of the first **provisional American cemetery** in the Cotentin Peninsula (/// misfortunes.relit.qualify). Between 1944 and 1948, some 6,000 American servicemen were buried here, before being returned home or moved to the American cemetery at Colleville-sur-Mer (page 67).

La Fière and Chef-du-Pont Blocking German forces from counter-attacking Sainte-Mère-Église and Utah Beach from the west was a major objective on D-Day, and bridges were the key. In particular, two small bridges and causeways over the Merderet River at La Fière and Chef-du-Pont had to be quickly captured and held by US Airborne forces in order to prevent a German counter-attack, and later to provide crossing points for American armoured forces when they arrived. At La Fière, the Germans had let the river overspill on to its floodplain. Around 680 paratroopers from the 82nd Airborne Division, destined for a drop zone on the west bank of the Merderet, came down in the flooded area. The marshy water was 1–2.5m deep, but more than 100 paratroopers, weighed down by almost 60 kilos of equipment, and without the quick-release buckles used by British paratroopers, are thought to have drowned. Thirty-six bodies were later recovered.

A three-day battle took place at La Fière, with 254 US soldiers killed and 545 wounded. Today, a **memorial park** has been established on the hillside overlooking the small stone bridge (junction of La Fière road & D15). The main monument is an **Iron Mike statue** (Iron Mike is American slang for standout soldiers). This larger-than-life-size depiction of a US paratrooper, casually holding his Thompson submachine gun as he looks out towards Cauquigny Church at the far end of the causeway, names Brigadier General James Gavin, who led from the front at this battle. Nearby, an extraordinary panoramic map explains the layout of the battlefield. Among other plaques in the park dedicated to individual units and soldiers, a small patch of ground about 80m up the track from the car park is marked as a foxhole that Gavin used during the battle.

Half a kilometre west of the bridge along the D15, the little, stone, 12th-century **Cauquigny Church** still shows signs of battle damage, including a bullet crater on a stone cross in the churchyard. Inside, there is information and photos showing how this unassuming spot was at the centre of the battle for the river crossing. By the road there is a stele to the **325th Glider Infantry Regiment** (GIR; cnr of D15 & rue Ham aux Brix), in the shape of a glider wing complete with black-and-white invasion stripes (on the eve of the invasion, to minimise the risk of friendly fire, every Allied aircraft had these stripes painted on its wings). The 325th GIR were at the heart of the assault to retake the river crossing.

Southwest on D15, 400m from Cauquigny Church, is a memorial to **Private First Class Charles DeGlopper** of the 325th GIR (/// manned.decibel.stepladder). DeGlopper, from Grand Island, New York, already stood out among his comrades when he first joined up: they had problems finding a uniform and boots to fit his 2.1m, 109kg frame. Aged 22, he had already fought in north Africa by the time of D-Day. His company was charged with taking the causeway over the Merderet River in the early hours of 9 June, but a group of soldiers got separated in the darkness and emerged on to a nearby road to find themselves facing superior German forces on three sides. While most of the men retreated through the hedge, DeGlopper began firing his Browning automatic rifle to draw attention away and allow his comrades to escape. He was wounded almost immediately but continued to fire, dropping to his knee when he was hit a second time, before eventually succumbing to his wounds. For his heroic self-sacrifice he was posthumously presented America's highest award, the Medal of Honor. The tall black stele here has an etched image of DeGlopper firing his gun from the hip. There's also a small marker to him in La Fière memorial park (page 93).

West of La Fière by 1.8km, on the D126, there is a small park (by the junction with D130) where gravel paths lead to different stones and tribute markers, each with a tale to tell. The main monument, 'The Beginning', is a tall carved stone relief of a paratrooper holding on to his parachute, representing the **507th PIR**, with a list of campaigns the regiment has fought in and the commendations it has won. Two 2m-high grey obelisks have details of their campaigns in the Ardennes (Battle of the Bulge), and Operation Varsity (airborne landings across the Rhine into Germany). A simple rough headstone, with an etched portrait, commemorates **Private Second Class Joe Gandara** of the 507th's D Company, who was posthumously awarded the Medal of Honor for his actions on 9 June. When his detachment came under heavy fire near the hamlet of La Pesquerie 1.5km north of this park, Gandara single-handedly rushed the enemy with his 30-calibre submachine gun and put three enemy guns out of action, before being killed by a German sniper.

Down a small gravel lane, in the middle of nowhere, three large stone blocks are laid out on gravel in front of a low hedge and an orchard (2.4km from La Fière; rte du Tiers; /// catchers.unanimously.grandson). The large centre block is dedicated to **Lieutenant Colonel Charles J Timmes** and his men of the 2nd Battalion, 507th PIR. On 6 June, Timmes landed in 60cm of water and was nearly drowned by his parachute dragging him down. He recovered and spent the next two days, with around 100 men, fighting off superior numbers of Germans in the orchard. Finally he established contact with the 82nd Airborne Division HQ and was sent a battalion from the 325th GIR as reinforcements. On 9 June he started attacking the Germans at Cauquigny and La Fière causeway. His dogged defence was well noted and, in another action on 3 July near Le Haye-du-Puits on the west side of the Cotentin, his heroism and leadership, under attack from superior forces, earned him the Distinguished Service Cross (DSC). In addition to the DSC, his decorations by the time he retired from service in 1967 included two Distinguished Service Medals, the Silver Star, two Bronze Stars and two Purple Hearts. The two smaller blocks honour the 507th PIR and the 325th GIR. Information boards explain the roles played by Timmes and Brigadier General James Gavin, who landed nearby.

Heading south of La Fière, 2.4km away, there is a memorial to **Captain Ignatius P Maternowski** (by 371–374 Gueutteville, just off D15). In the early hours of 6 June, many paratroopers of the 508th PIR were scattered around the small hamlet of Gueutteville, which was garrisoned by German, Georgian and Mongolian troops of the 1,057th Infantry Regiment, 91st Division. Some paratroopers went to a French café to seek directions and pretty quickly wounded paratroopers began to gather here. The café became an aid station and the senior officer, Father Maternowski – a catholic chaplain with the 508th PIR – showed incredible bravery

1 The Higgins Boat memorial outside the Utah Beach Landing Museum. 2 The Utah Beach Landing Museum houses a Douglas B-26 Marauder twin-engined bomber, one of only six left in the world. 3 Sainte-Marie-du-Mont's French Resistance statue. 4 Sainte-Mère-Église's church has a model of paratrooper John Steele dangling from his parachute. 5 On board a glider at the Airborne Museum. ▸

BILL PERRY/S

COLLECTION MUSÉE UTAH BEACH

ALASTAIR MCKENZIE

ANDRE MULLER/S

AIRBORNE MUSEUM

by walking through the village unarmed to speak to the German commanding officer, to ask him to recognise the café and another building as non-combatant medical facilities under the Geneva Convention. Amazingly, he wasn't shot and the German officer returned with him to check the buildings and the condition of the wounded. Afterwards, Father Maternowski escorted the officer back to the upper part of the hamlet, but as he was returning to the aid station he was shot in the back and killed. It's not clear whether a sniper shot him, or maybe the officer himself. This remembrance spot, with its etched image of Father Maternowski giving the last rites to a dying soldier, is located next to the spot on the road where he died.

The bridge over the Merderet River at **Chef-du-Pont**, a village southeast of La Fière and 4.5km southwest of Sainte-Mère-Église, was a critical crossing point. On D-Day, elements of the 507th and 508th PIRs of the 82nd Airborne Division fought hard to capture the village and the bridge and then hold them against fierce counter-attacks. At one point Captain Roy E Creek, commander of E Company, 507th PIR, was down to 20 men before reinforcements arrived. Just north of the bridge, by the side of the D70 (/// observation.minimalist.reversal), a tall cobbled stone remembers the **508th PIR**, and opposite there is a small remembrance garden gifted by 508th veterans. The bridge was later renamed after **Captain Roy Creek**, and on the bank of the river just by the bridge, a board has a photograph of him taken on the spot in 2000. He died in 2016.

Picauville and around Picauville was one of the first towns liberated by Allied airborne forces (by the US 9th Air Force, 10 June), but the number of aircraft memorials in and around Picauville bears witness to the ferocity of German AA fire. Those C-47 transport aircraft that flew under the cloud experienced the worst casualties – while those that flew above the clouds ended up scattering their paratroopers up to 15km from their intended drop zones.

In the town centre, in the car park opposite the church, a wall with plaques commemorates the crews of four **C-47s of the 50th and 53rd troop carrier wings**, which crashed around Picauville (5 rue de l'Eglise). To the right of the remembrance wall, a glass case contains the wrecked engine of one of those C-47s. To the left a concrete stone remembers all the USAAF and RAF units who flew from the nearby A-8N ALG (page 52), and the names of the 19 pilots who were killed while the airfield was operational.

Three of the four aircraft also have memorials at their crash sites. Heading northeast of the town along La Chevalerie road, there is a memorial garden (/// refrigerate.successfully.finest), which – surrounded by trees – is an oasis of calm. It marks the spot where a C-47 of the **91st Troop Carrier Squadron**, 50th Troop Carrier Wing, was hit by AA fire and crashed in the early hours of 6 June. The crew of four and the 16 paratroopers from 506th PIR it was carrying were killed instantly. Around the garden are named plaques on the ground in front of sapling trees, which have been planted for each of those killed, and in the middle a near-life-size outline of a C-47 is marked out in grey slate.

East of Picauville, a simple metal plaque on the wall of a cottage (432 Founecrop; /// feed.thankfully.debility) marks the spot where the C-47 of the **77th Troop Carrier Squadron**, also of the 50th Wing, came down on D-Day, killing four crew and 17 paratroopers from the 501st PIR. And to the south, a plaque on a cottage wall, in the hamlet of Clainville (20 Clainville; /// ignore.cuckoos.recitals) shows exactly where another C-47 of the **77th Troop Carrier Squadron** came down, killing five crew and 14 501st PIR paratroopers, but – on this occasion – there were three survivors.

There were also a couple of advanced landing grounds near Picauville. **A-14 ALG** is marked with a simple grey headstone with gold lettering (junction between D267 & an unnamed lane into the village of Houtteville; /// flexes.hotels.contributing). The runway was on the other side of the D267 road and the marker remembers the 819th Engineer Aviation Battalion who built it, and the 358th and 406th fighter groups (flying P-47 Thunderbolts) who were based here from 3 July to 14 August. The southwestern end of the airfield was in the grounds of the magnificent **Château de Franquetot** (rue de Francquetot/D223, south of Cretteville; /// slang.hubs. diamond), where some of the officers were billeted. If you go to the main gate of the château, you'll find a further two plaques, on either side of the gate, to those two fighter groups again. Spare a thought then for the men of the 393rd Fighter Squadron (P-38 Lightnings) who also served on this ALG from 27 July to 15 August but are not remembered at either location. There are two châteaux de Franquetot in this neck of the woods – the other, 12.5km northeast, was the HQ of General Joe Collins (page 92) and is more like fortified farm.

A-8N ALG (where the N designation denotes an airfield equipped for night operations) is marked with a simple grey headstone with gold lettering at the side of the road (D69, Étienville; 300m south of D130 junction; /// gown.cheapens.pencil). It is dedicated to all those who lost their lives working or flying from here. A-8N, constructed by the 826th Engineer Aviation Battalion, was the base for the 405th Fighter Group (P-47 Thunderbolts) from 30 June to 14 September 1944, and the 264th and 604th RAF night fighter squadrons (Mosquitoes) between 6 August and 8 September.

North of Sainte-Mère-Église

Orglandes German military cemetery (Rue Pierre Devouassoud/D24; 7km west of Sainte-Mère-Église; /// alleged.runes.meandering; ⏰ 09.00–17.00 daily; free; ♿) On the northern edge of the village of Orglandes, this spacious cemetery (5ha) feels lighter and more open than other German cemeteries in Normandy, but it's just as densely packed. Each 50cm-tall stone cross marks the final resting places of up to six deceased soldiers. In total, 10,155 soldiers are buried here. As the Americans advanced on Cherbourg, both German and American dead were buried here, but after 1945 the Americans were moved to the Colleville-sur-Mer cemetery (page 67), and the French authorities began to consolidate German graves in Orglandes.

Airship Hangar Museum (Musée Hangar à Dirigeables; La Bazirerie, Écausseville; ☎ 02 33 08 56 02; w aerobase.fr; ⏰ Feb 14.00–18.00 French school holidays; Apr–Jun & Sep–mid-Nov 14.00–18.00 daily; Jul–Aug 10.00–18.00 daily; adult/child €6.00/2.50; ♿ but gravel paths to negotiate) A huge domed airship hangar, in the middle of farmland 10km northwest of Sainte-Mère-Église, is clearly visible from the surrounding roads. It is a legacy from World War I, one of two built at the Montebourg Naval Airship Base (page 98) between 1917 and 1919 to accommodate anti-submarine airships. While the second hanger was built of wood and has not survived, this colossal hanger – 140m long, 40m wide and 32m high – was built of reinforced concrete. In World War II both the Germans and the Americans used it as a storage depot and, in the case of the Americans, as a heavy vehicle maintenance depot and temporary POW camp. The small, packed museum in a building next to it covers the history of the base and the local area under occupation and liberation; if you can, talk to the ex-pilot who runs it: he's very knowledgeable. Outside, a short circular walk through the field to the hanger entrance takes you past a memorial to local citizens who died during the war and the **4th Infantry Division** and **325th Glider Regiment** who captured the hangar between 8 and 10 June 1944.

Azeville Battery (La rue, Azeville; ✆02 33 40 63 05; w batterie-azeville.manche. fr; ⊕ 6 Feb–7 Apr & 23 Sep–11 Nov 13.00–18.00 Sun–Thu; 8 Apr–7 Jul & 1–22 Sep 09.00–18.30 daily (except 1 May); 8 Jul–31 Aug 09.30–19.00 daily; adult/child €8/4) It's now surrounded by trees and vegetation, but in June 1944, Azeville Battery, up on a headland, looked towards the sea. The battery is unusual: its four large casemates with 105mm guns (no longer there) were built 5km inland after an open battery on the coast was put out of action by a large storm in February 1942. Not only could it cover a large portion of the coast but, with widened embrasures, it could also traverse its gun far enough to disrupt the progress of Allied forces as they worked their way inland. The German garrison of 173 men was not a crack unit – they were drawn from all over Germany and the territories it had annexed, with an average age of 34 and the oldest soldier being 54. Nevertheless, despite being attacked on 6 June by some stray airborne troops, and then more seriously by land forces from 7 June, they managed to hold out until 9 June. A network of underground tunnels, some of which you can explore, link the casemates with defensive pillboxes, stores and barracks. Look out for the renovated camouflage painted on two of the bunkers, designed to make them look like innocent houses. There's also some dramatic battle damage: on 7 June the battleship USS *Nevada* managed to hit one casemate with a pair of 35cm shells. One exploded on the southeast corner, while the other flew in through the embrasure, crashed through the back wall into the gun crew room behind, failed to explode and passed back outside through the next wall. Some say the shock wave killed all 15 men in the crew room; others say five men were killed. Either way, it put the casemate out of action, and you can still see the devastating holes it made.

Crisbecq Battery (Rte de Crisbecq, Saint-Marcouf; m 06 68 41 09 04; w batterie-marcouf.com; ⊕ Apr–Jun & Sep–mid-Nov 10.00–18.00 daily; Jul–Aug 10.00–19.00 daily; last ticket 1hr before closing; adult/child €10.50/6.50) High on a hill, with a commanding view over flat fields and the sea to the north, Crisbecq was unlike other major coastal batteries in Normandy, in that it didn't follow the usual German pattern of four casemates for its main armament. Instead it had two large casemates (and a third under construction) for three 210mm Skoda guns, and six open gun pits for a range of other artillery. The Crisbecq Battery Museum grounds cover the six open gun pits, one of the large casemates and a set of bunkers, with a numbered trail to follow through them. The bunkers were built for ammunition, food and equipment stores, mess rooms, barracks, an infirmary and defensive machine-gun and AA emplacements. The second 210mm casemate, **Marcouf 44**, just down the hill (rte des Manoirs), is also open to the public. The German soldiers left the Crisbecq Battery on 11 June. The **Command Post bunker** (Musée Poste de

Commandement des Batteries; rte de Crisbecq; m 06 76 16 56 75; w crisbecq44.fr; ⊕ Jun–Aug; adult/child €12/6) is on the other side of the main road. It is privately owned but the owner sometimes allows visits – telephone in advance.

Northwest of the battery, a small stone stele with a red sandstone plaque (west of rte de Fontenay/D14; /// growers.spaceships.vitality) marks the site of **A-7 ALG** and pays tribute to the 365th Fighter Group (P-47 Thunderbolts), based here from 28 June to 15 August, the 363rd (P-51 Mustangs), based here from 22 August and 14 September, and the 819th Engineer Aviation Battalion, who built the landing ground.

World War II Museum (18 av de la Plage, Quinéville; ☏ 02 33 95 95 95; w worldwar2-museum.com; ⊕ Apr & Sep–6 Nov 10.00–18.00 daily, May–Aug 10.00–19.00 daily, last tickets 1hr before closing; adult/child €9/6; ♿) This museum, built on to the back of a beach defence bunker, includes vehicles, equipment, and 1:6-scale models covering the occupation and D-Day landings. The dioramas are particularly good for families: it feels as if you are walking through a giant doll's house.

Saint-Germain-de-Varreville This village, 6km northeast of Sainte-Mère-Église, includes a grey headstone-style monument honouring the **US 101st Airborne Division Pathfinders** (D14–D129 junction), who landed here at 00.16 on 6 June. Arriving in three C-47 transport aircraft, Pathfinder Team A of 502nd PIR, along with ten Pathfinders from 377th Parachute Field Artillery Regiment, were not quite the first to land on D-Day (as the information panels suggest), since Major Howard's glider landed at Pegasus Bridge at 00.11 (page 21), but close enough. The Pathfinders quickly set up Holophane beacon lights in the shape of a T in the field behind the fortified farm opposite to guide other paratroopers in, and 101st Airborne paratroopers began landing here from 00.57. You can get a view of the field from the town hall car park. Note also the trees of the churchyard opposite the town hall: the Pathfinders set up three Eureka radar transponders in those trees. The wall of the fortified farm has two more information panels: one remembers two leaders of the Pathfinders, while the other celebrates the Free French 2nd Armoured Division driving through the village on their way to Sainte-Mère-Église (page 90).

North of the village, along the D14, in a peaceful, rural spot among the fields, information boards mark the location of a huge temporary **German prisoner-of-war camp** (/// slated.built.unready) that once stood here. It was the size of a small town, housing up to 40,000 German POWs including 218 generals and six admirals. Built at the end of June 1944 by American engineers and German soldiers, it had an extraordinary range of facilities: a 1,000-bed hospital, a football ground, a 400-seat theatre and ballroom for US soldiers, and an 860-seat theatre for the POWs. The camp was almost self-sufficient for vegetables, with 40ha of land, and had its own water supply, electricity and several kilometres of narrow-gauge railway, with 75 wagons pulled by diesel and petrol engines that could distribute rations in 45 minutes. Perhaps it isn't surprising that no POWs tried to escape. The camp was demolished in early 1947, when all the prisoners had been released or relocated.

CHERBOURG AND THE CENTRAL COTENTIN PENINSULA

Cherbourg, at the northernmost end of the Cotentin Peninsula, has always held a vital strategic position in France. From 1900 onwards it was one of the main harbours for the liners that crossed the Atlantic; in 1944 it inevitably became one of the ports that the Allies had to take, and take quickly; the 'Great Storm' of 19 June had just wiped out the Mulberry A Harbour at Omaha.

The 20,000 German soldiers defending the city, a mélange of poor-grade and undertrained troops, were completely cut off, with no hope of re-supply or rescue. They were under the usual orders from Hitler: not to let Cherbourg fall and to defend to the last bullet.

The Allied attack was launched with a bombing raid at 14.00 on 22 June. Progress was steady for the next two days as US troops methodically worked their way through the outskirts of Cherbourg. Groups of Germans defended as best they could under an overwhelming aerial, artillery and tank bombardment from all directions, and then inevitably surrendered. At midday on 25 June, three battleships, four cruisers and nine destroyers joined the bombardment. When they withdrew three and a half hours later, they had fired over 3,000 shells. Finally, on 26 June, the remaining German troops were holed up in a tunnel under the cliffs at Fort du Roule. A few tank rounds into the entrances of the side tunnels was all it took for a general, an admiral and 840 men to surrender.

Cherbourg was heavily damaged by the bombing. In the post-war years much of the city was rebuilt, but its old buildings were not restored; today its main attraction is the superb Cité de la Mer (City of the Sea) Museum, housed in the former Transatlantic liner terminal, which features *Le Redoutable*, France's first nuclear missile submarine, and a special exhibition on the *Titanic*, which stopped at Cherbourg on its way from Southampton to New York, on 10 April 1912. But there are also some important D-Day sites looking down on the city.

GETTING THERE AND AROUND Cherbourg is one of the main ports for **ferries** from the UK and Ireland (page 5). You can also **drive** there from the other ferry ports (page 5). **Trains** leave regularly from Bayeux (1hr 11mins) and from Caen, via Bayeux (1hr 41mins). Regular, direct trains also run from Paris Saint-Lazare (3hrs 15mins). By bus, take the 301 from Carentan (5/day; approx 1hr 11mins). Cherbourg is a busy town with some serious hills. It's best to have a **car** or take a **tour**.

TOURIST INFORMATION

Cherbourg tourist information office 56 quai de Caligny; ☏ 08 05 32 02 00; w encotentin. fr/cherbourg; ⏲ Jul–Aug 09.30–12.30 & 13.30–18.30 daily; Sep–Jun 09.30–12.30 & 13.30–18.00 Mon–Sat

Bricquebec-en-Cotentin tourist information office 13 pl Sainte-Anne; ☏ 08 05 32 02 00; w encotentin.fr/ bricquebec-en-cotentin; ⏲ Jul–mid-Sep 10.00–12.30 & 14.00–18.00 Mon–Fri

WHAT TO SEE AND DO

Fort du Roule This 19th-century fortress was built, under Napoleon III, to defend Cherbourg from the English. At 117m above sea level, it enjoys spectacular views over the port. Part of the hilltop site, which is reachable only up a zig-zag mountain road from the city, is still used by the French military. However, the old fortress is now the home of the **Cherbourg Liberation Museum**

1 The Pyramid of Memory in Bricquebec-en-Cotentin is slowly eroding to reveal finds from Utah Beach. 2 The memorial garden in Picauville includes a near-life-size outline of a C-47 transport aircraft. 3 The D-Day Collins Museum faithfully recreates US General Joe Lawton Collins's office, with accurate models of Collins with Eisenhower and Lieutenant General Omar Bradley. 4 Headstones in Orglandes German cemetery each mark the graves of up to six soldiers. ▶

UWE ZUCCHI FOR VOLKSBUND DT. KRIEGSGRÄBERFÜRSORGE

(Musée de la Libération; montée des Résistants; 📞 02 33 20 14 12; w cherbourg.
fr/infos-services/culture-et-loisirs/musees/musee-de-la-liberation-321.html;
🕐 10.00–12.30 & 14.00–18.00 Tue–Fri, 13.00–18.00 Sat–Sun; adult/under-26 €5/
free), which is worth a visit just for the view alone. Housed on several levels, the
museum uses simple stylised dioramas, historic photographs, posters, audio and
personal artefacts to tell the story of Cherbourg's occupation and liberation. It is
both an interesting and poignant display, and there's an excellent film about the
liberation and residents' suffering, made in 1954, which has footage you won't see
in other museums.

The clifftop tunnels underneath the fortress hide the German **Batterie du Roule**
(montée des Résistants, one zig-zag down from the fortress; m 06 31 45 25 80;
w exspen.com/batterie-du-roule; 🕐 1 or 2 small-group guided tours a day, must
be pre-booked by phone or text; hours & days vary, check website; adult/10–18yrs/
under-10s €12/9/6). In 1928, the French navy dug an extensive network of tunnels
in the mountain under the fortress for use as stores. When the Germans occupied
Cherbourg in June 1940, they started constructing four casemates in the tunnels
for 105mm guns. Despite machine gun, mortar and AA defences above and around
the tunnel battery, it was speedily captured by US 79th Infantry Division on 26
June 1944. The tours, which last around 90 minutes, take visitors approximately
1km underground.

Heading south from Cherbourg

Brix This village, 12km south of Cherbourg, has a **memorial area** (rue des
Forges/D50, near the junction with D119) to commemorate the loss of a USAAF
B-17 Flying Fortress bomber with all its crew near here on 20 April 1944, as well as
the pilot of a P-47 Thunderbolt on 17 June. The B-17, from 568th Bomb Squadron
based at Framlingham in Suffolk, were hit by AA fire just after dropping their
bombs on the Cherbourg area, spinning out of control with one engine and a
wing on fire; a 1.5m-high stone edifice lists the names of the ten crew who died.
Close by is the wrecked engine of the P-47 in a glass cabinet, with its damaged
propeller lying next to it, as a tribute to pilot Lieutenant Gary Lewis Gray of 513th
Fighter-Bomber Squadron, another victim of AA fire. One of his fellow pilots
saw him bail out, and locals on the ground saw him land, but were later told he
had been shot by German soldiers. He is buried at the American Cemetery in
Colleville-sur-Mer (page 67).

Bricquebec-en-Cotentin In the town of Bricquebec-en-Cotentin, 23.5km
south of Cherbourg, there is a weathered copper **sculpture of a B-17 bomber** (cnr
of Le Foyer/D902 & D519) dramatically spiralling down to earth, with its tail and
one wing torn off. It remembers two bomber crews who met their fate nearby:
one was shot down over Rocheville on 27 April 1944; the other was shot down
over Bricquebec on 8 May. Tragically, the pilot and tail gunner were on their final
mission before going home, and the ball-turret gunner had already completed his
mission quota and wasn't supposed to be flying.

In the public gardens of the town's château (pl le Marois; now a hotel & restaurant)
the **Pyramid of Memory**, by French sculptor Pascal Morabito – unveiled on 31
December 1999, to mark the Millennium – has 2000 objects from the 20th century
buried inside, many of them relating to the invasion. Its actual form is a concrete
octahedron, but as half of it is buried, what remains is a pyramid. The concrete is
made from sand from Utah Beach and it is not strong – the idea is that it slowly
erodes, revealing the objects inside gradually. At the time of research, the base of

After his victories in Tunisia (1942) and then Sicily (1943), the German high command considered US General George S Patton to be the most capable Allied tank tactician and therefore the 'one to watch'. Unfortunately for the Germans, the Allies exploited that view by using Patton to distract them, and then pummel them.

Patton had earned a reputation in World War I as a skilled and innovative cavalry officer. In the interwar years, he became a strong advocate for armoured warfare and was instrumental in developing the US Army's tank corps and tactics.

However, Patton was a controversial figure. He could be ruthless with those who didn't match his standards. An incident in Sicily in August 1943, when he slapped two shell-shocked soldiers, resulted in him losing command of the 7th Army and being sent back to England in disgrace. There he was ostentatiously put in command of a new, wholly fictitious army mustering in Kent, the closest point to Pas-de-Calais where the Germans fully expected the Allies' most dangerous general to lead an invasion.

Meanwhile, the core of a new army, the US 3rd Army, was being formed in secret outside Knutsford in Cheshire, and in March 1944, Patton took command of its 253,500 men. The 3rd Army was moved to France during July 1944, and assembled outside Néhou. It became officially operational on 1 August when the Operation Cobra breakout from Saint-Lô reached Avranches and General Patton was unleashed. Doing what he did best, and the Germans feared most, Patton drove his divisions southwest into Brittany and then east at breakneck speed, trapping the Germans in the Falaise Pocket, before moving on to Paris. Despite the controversies, Patton, who survived the war, was an inspiring leader. He once said: 'An army is like a piece of cooked spaghetti. You can't push it, you have to pull it after you.'

a 105mm brass shell casing, a bullet clip and what looked like two hand grenades were among the visible objects. A notice asks that visitors take any objects that become detached to the town hall, to be preserved in the museum.

Camp Patton memorial park (Rue de la Belle Manière, Néhou; ⏰ 24hrs daily) General George S Patton (see above) arrived in Normandy on 6 July, a month after D-Day, and set up his HQ just outside the town of Néhou. US troops gathered secretly in the surrounding fields over the following weeks, and on 2 August Patton was given command of the 3rd Army. The park, with an M4A1 Sherman tank as a 'gate guardian', has a number of monuments and photographic displays of officers who were camped here with Patton. The orchard at the back is where the general had his personal trailer-caravan and Command Post tent. Only one apple tree in the centre of the field bore witness to the events; the rest were replanted in 1993.

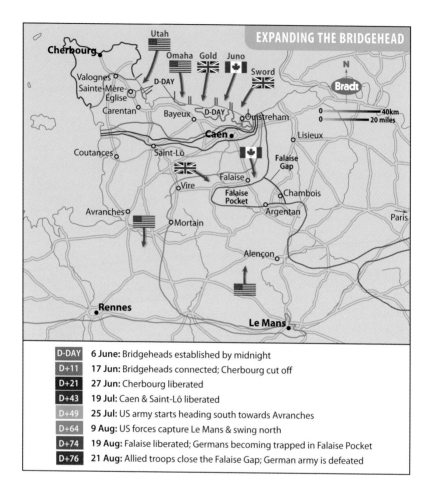

EXPANDING THE BRIDGEHEAD

D-DAY	**6 June:** Bridgeheads established by midnight
D+11	**17 Jun:** Bridgeheads connected; Cherbourg cut off
D+21	**27 Jun:** Cherbourg liberated
D+43	**19 Jul:** Caen & Saint-Lô liberated
D+49	**25 Jul:** US army starts heading south towards Avranches
D+64	**9 Aug:** US forces capture Le Mans & swing north
D+74	**19 Aug:** Falaise liberated; Germans becoming trapped in Falaise Pocket
D+76	**21 Aug:** Allied troops close the Falaise Gap; German army is defeated

Part Three

EXPANDING THE BRIDGEHEAD

Saint-Lô and the Bocage

Getting through the defences on the beaches on 6 June was hard enough but, as the Allies moved inland, many of them began to encounter the tricky terrain of the bocage. Bocage is a Norman word that describes a rural landscape of woods and small fields bordered by thick hedgerows growing from earth embankments, which makes them very solid, with sunken lanes in between. This kind of landscape is not unique (for example, the sunken lanes of Devon), but it is uniquely difficult to traverse and uniquely easy to defend; the enemy can lie in wait behind every hedge. In Normandy the bocage runs in a wide swathe from the Cotentin Peninsula southeast to Falaise. It took over eight weeks for the Allies to break through the bocage into open landscapes.

When XIX Corps of the US 1st Army, led by the 29th Infantry Division, headed towards the key communications centre of Saint-Lô, it was a month of slow and painful movement. They lost thousands of men as they inched forward through the bocage, before finally taking the bombed-out remains of Saint-Lô on 19 July. As one American soldier put it: 'We sure liberated the hell out of this place.'

Meanwhile the British were also battling their way through the bocage. At the end of July the British 2nd Army's VIII Corps was fighting for hilltops and river crossings around Saint-Martin des-Besaces as part of Operation Bluecoat (page 116).

This whole area is rich and fertile and very pretty to drive through... unless, of course, you are fighting a war. One interesting aspect of this area today is the number of small, off-the-beaten-track museums to visit, such as the excellent little Liberation Memorial Museum in Périers.

SAINT-LÔ

The medieval walled city of Saint-Lô, on the banks of the Vire River, suffered badly in 1944, right from the start of the invasion. Its location at a major crossroads at the bottom of the Cotentin Peninsula made it a critical target for the Allies. On the night of 6–7 June the city was heavily bombed, bringing down one of the two soaring steeples of the

SAINT-LÔ AND THE BOCAGE

○ **Memorials**

13th-century Notre Dame Church and destroying the prison. Then, in mid-July, it was again bombed and shelled over three days as US XIX Corps (29th, 30th and 35th Infantry Divisions) fought the German 352nd Infantry Division and 2nd Parachute Corps to capture it. The long-suffering Notre Dame Church was hit by a 100mm brass shell that is still embedded in the wall of its nave (at about head height, on the cobbled rue Carnot). With over 97% of its buildings damaged or destroyed, Saint-Lô became known as the 'capital of ruins' (page 109).

After the war a major restoration programme got underway. Historic buildings were patched up or rebuilt. The stone ramparts and towers that had protected the city from the time of Charlemagne to Napoleon, but not from the US Air Force, were rebuilt and are now a listed historical monument, as are the Magdalen Chapel,

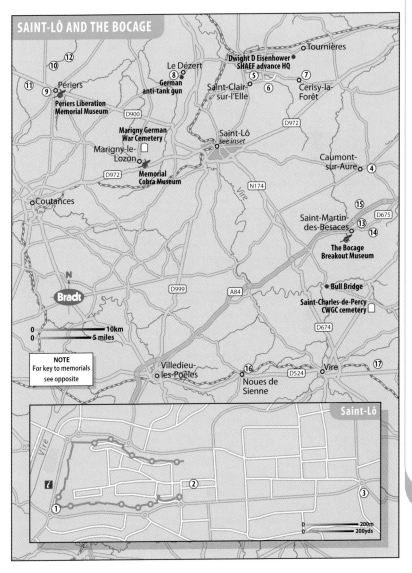

the Holy Cross Church, and Château de la Vaucelle, a former residence of three kings: Edward III, Francis I and Charles IX.

Now the city has a new name: 'The capital of the horse.' Saint-Lô is home to the National Stud Farm, one of the largest in France. The farm's buildings, which are also listed, were originally built in 1882–90 and were rebuilt as precise replicas after the war. On Thursdays from the end of July to September, visitors can see the splendid stallions.

There is a **tourist information office** in the centre (60 rue de la Poterne; 02 14 29 00 17; w saintlo-tourisme.fr; year-round, hours vary; check website).

GETTING THERE AND AROUND Saint-Lô is easily reached from the **ferry** ports (page 5) by travelling via Bayeux or Caen. It lies 30km southwest of Bayeux and, if **driving**, is reached by the E3 and D572 roads running south from the N13. There are regular **trains** from Bayeux (30mins), Caen (50mins), Cherbourg (2hrs 6mins, with a change at Bayeux), and Paris Saint-Lazare (3hrs 8mins, changing at either Caen or Lison). There is no **bus** from Caen or Bayeux to Saint-Lô; you have to go to Bayeux and take the train.

Saint-Lô is relatively compact and there are buses within the town. To see the sites around Saint-Lô, you need a car or to take a **tour**.

WHAT TO SEE AND DO
Monument to the bombing victims (Monument à la mémoire des victimes du bombardement, prom André Hilt, above D999) The huge monument on the side of a hill is a sombre sight, commemorating the civilians who died or were injured first in the Allied bombing of 6–7 June, when the first American airstrike alone killed around 800 civilians, then in further bombing by both the Germans and the Allies in which a further 352 were killed. Saint-Lô received France's military award the Croix de Guerre on 2 June 1948, for the way in which the city 'suffered… with a heroic calm, an air bombardment to such a point that its inhabitants could consider themselves citizens of the capital of the ruins'.

Saint-Lô Prison (Pl Général de Gaulle) All that is left of the substantial 19th-century prison is a large semi-circular porch and the remains of walls to each side. On the night of 6–7 June, Allied bombing hit the prison and the German guards fled the city, leaving 200 prisoners, many of them members of the Resistance, to die. An urn by the old wooden door contains ashes of the dead prisoners. Names on both walls remember local people (including whole families) shot or deported by the Nazis. A newer marble stone to the left remembers local troops involved in the Indochina and Korean conflicts. To the people of Saint-Lô, this is a significant monument; there are always wreaths or flowers or dedications placed at the site.

The Major of Saint-Lô memorial (Rue du Rossignol, by pl du Major Howie D974 roundabout) A large, semi-circular monument honours Major Thomas D Howie, commander of the 3rd Battalion, 29th Infantry Division, who was killed by shrapnel on 17 July during the Battle of Saint-Lô. An inscription beneath a bust of Howie reads: 'He fell at the head of his troops as he was liberating our city. His last words were: "To Saint-Lô". The following day, as American troops moved into the city, the 29th Infantry Division's commander, Major General Charles H Gerhardt,

◀ 1 & 2 The bocage region of Normandy is a maze of small fields, hedgerows and sunken lanes that hampered the Allied advance, with woodland providing perfect cover for defending German troops.

ordered his body to be carried on the hood of the first jeep so that he would be the first American to enter Saint-Lô. Draped with a flag, his body was put on the rubble of the old Sainte-Croix Church, enabling soldiers and citizens to pay their respects. A photograph of his flag-draped corpse became one of the iconic images of American sacrifice in World War II. Howie is buried at the American Cemetery at Colleville-sur-Mer (page 67).

NORTH AND EAST OF SAINT-LÔ

There are a number of good museums and memorials commemorating the Allies' advance through the bocage to Saint-Lô.

MEMORIALS In the town of Caumont-sur-Aure, 22km east of Saint-Lô, a simple white headstone in the grounds of Église Saint-Clair et Saint-Martin marks the town's liberation on 13 June by the **US 1st Infantry Division** ('Big Red One', page 69). North of the village of Saint-Clair-sur-l'Elle, 13km from Saint-Lô, there is a **memorial garden to the US 29th Infantry Division** (Le Pont de la Pierre; /// welding.ulcer.outdone; ☺ 10.00–19.00 daily; free). A simple white stone topped with the insignia of the 'Blue and Gray' division, which stands by the small Elle stream, records the names of those 16 soldiers killed here on 12 June. Saint-Claire-sur-l'Elle was liberated late in the evening of 13 June. The division is also honoured with a **wall of remembrance** in the town of Saint-Jean-de-Savigny (4.4km east of Saint-Clair-sur-l'Elle; by the junction of D54 & D59; /// copied.choker.meal), covered in commemorative plaques.

Continuing east, in Cerisy-la-Forêt village 9.5km away, there is an unusual but stylish memorial to the **US 2nd Infantry Division** (junction of rue Jean Gremillon & av Deuxième Division). A stone sculpture resembles an indigenous American headdress, commemorating the 'Indianheads' – the division's nickname, which it gained in World War I when the symbol was adopted as its insignia. After landing in Saint-Laurent-sur-Mer on Omaha Beach on 6 June (page 71), the division, led by General Robertson, liberated Trévières on 10 June, then Cerisy-la-Forêt on the same day, and set up their command position in the village from 15 to 19 June. They then took Hill 192, 9km south near Cloville, which controlled the road to Saint-Lô.

Near Tournières, 4.5km north of Cerisy-la-Forêt, a simple stone down a small lane in the middle of farmland (Ballieul; /// long.outrage.familiarity) marks a once-significant position: this was where US General Dwight D Eisenhower set up his first **SHAEF advance HQ** (see opposite) on 7 August. A photo of Eisenhower walking with Free French General Charles de Gaulle hangs over the stone, which was inaugurated by members of the US government and the Eisenhower family 6 June 1990, the centennial anniversary year of his birth and the 46th anniversary of D-Day.

In the village of Le Dézert, 14km north of Saint-Lô, a 75mm **German anti-tank gun** (a PanzerAbwehrKanone 40) sits outside the town hall (pl de la Mairie). The four white rings on the gun indicate four 'kills', but it is not known when they were painted. Close by, on the wall of the town hall, a plaque pays homage to **Colonel Harry Flint** and his men of the US 39th Infantry Regiment, 9th Infantry Division, who died liberating the commune. Col Flint was shot by a sniper on 23 July and died the next day from his injuries.

PÉRIERS AND AROUND The charming little market town of Périers (30km northwest of Saint-Lô) is at the junction of five roads. There used to be a railway

At any one time it was possible for there to be more than one SHAEF. Eisenhower's 'main' SHAEF HQ, with its full staff, would follow advance parties rolling forward as the European campaign advanced. On D-Day the main SHAEF was in Bushy Park, London, and the 'forward' SHAEF, with Eisenhower's combat staff, was in Portsmouth, nearest to the troops. As soon as possible, a small 'advance' SHAEF was set up on the continent, at Tournières, which Eisenhower joined on 7 August. On 1 September Eisenhower moved his forward SHAEF to Jullouville, on the west coast of the Cotentin Peninsula, from where he took back direct command of the Allied forces from his ground commanders. On 20 September, the forward SHAEF moved to the Trianon Palace Hotel in Versailles, which the full staff from the main SHAEF HQ in London joined on 5 October. Meanwhile a small advance SHAEF had opened on 19 September at Gueux, near Reims, and the forward SHAEF moved into Reims itself on 17 February 1945. Three months later, on 7 May 1945, the Chief-of-Staff of German Forces, General Alfred Jodl, signed the unconditional surrender document there.

too, but it was closed in 1970 and the station is now the town library. In July 1944, the US 90th Infantry Division approached from the north through the bocage, but, on 14 July, were blocked by the 6th German Parachute (Fallschirmjäger) Regiment in the marshlands around the Sèves River. Fighting was fierce and it wasn't until 27 July that Périers was finally liberated.

To get there by **car** from Saint-Lô, take the D900 (31.2km; 32mins); from Cherbourg, take the N13 and D24 (58.8km; 55mins); and the N13 and D971 will get you there from Bayeux (61.6km; 51mins) or Ouistreham (108km; 1hr 15mins).

The nearest **tourist information offices** are in Lessay (Côte Ouest Manche Tourisme; 10km away; w tourisme-cocm.fr) and Saint-Lô (page 109).

What to see and do
Périers Liberation Memorial Museum (1 bis pl du Général de Gaulle; m 06 88 04 27 41, 06 62 12 29 09; w normandy44.fr; ⏰ Jun–Aug 09.30–12.30 & 14.00–18.00 Sat, 10.00–noon & 14.00–18.00 Sun; other times by appointment, call ahead; free; ♿ up two steps) This fascinating little museum, in a single room in one of the town hall buildings, displays small pieces of equipment, uniforms, personal items and other memorabilia, along with detailed accounts and first-hand testimony of the Battle of Périers and the two Allied bombing raids on the town. A mini-cinema shows six history videos of varying lengths, five of them dubbed in French and English, the sixth in French only. On the outside wall the official **liberation plaque** is dedicated to the 72 men of the US 90th Division who gave their lives to free the town.

Town centre memorials By the town hall you'll find one of Normandy's more interesting statues: the **90th Infantry Division 'Tough Ombres' monument** (Les Quatre Braves, pl du Général de Gaulle). It features four men, who were all real soldiers who died during the liberation of Périers, their faces reproduced faithfully by the sculptor Patrick Cottencin. They are Private 2nd Class Andrew Jackson Speese III, who is wounded and trying to stand again; Private 1st Class Virgil John Tangborn, who was killed rescuing a driver from his burning truck; Private 2nd Class Richard E Richtman, who was killed in the battle at Chemin de l'Hôpital (see below); and tank commander Staff Sergeant Tullio Micaloni, who is depicted urgently calling his platoon of Sherman tanks forward to assist. On 26 July, Micaloni and his crew literally drew the short straw and were committed to being the first tank to attempt to ford the Sèves River and relieve troops at Chemin de l'Hôpital. Just over the river they triggered a stack of anti-tank mines, blowing the tank over and killing all inside. All four of the Tough Ombres (the division's nickname comes from their insignia, the combined letters T and O, standing for Texas and Oklahoma where most men were recruited) are buried in the American Cemetery at Colleville-sur-Mer (page 67).

The small park behind the town hall includes the **Colonel William McConahey memorial tree** (/// monopolies.subordinate.signs). Colonel McConahey was the surgeon of the US 344th Field Artillery Battalion, 90th Infantry Division. As the plaque says, 'In the midst of chaos he stood by the oath, tending to friend and foe equally with determination and dedication'. McConahey continued as the battalion surgeon and survived the war. There is also a wrecked plane engine and propeller among a small copse (/// lynched.freed.describes), in memory of **US pilots Kitchens and Espy**. On 24 June 1944, four P-47 Thunderbolts of 508 Squadron, 404th Fighter Group, were returning to their base in England from a patrol over Avranches when two of the pilots, Benjamin F Kitchens and Bert Espy Jr, spotted enemy vehicles and peeled off to attack them. Afterwards, as they were manoeuvring to rejoin the others, they collided and crashed on the outskirts of Périers, and both died. Some 20 years later the wreck of Espy's plane was unearthed, and on 24 June 2017, 73 years to the day after the crash, this memorial featuring its engine and propeller was inaugurated, in the presence of Kitchens' niece.

Chemin de l'Hôpital memorials The Chemin de l'Hôpital is a footpath that runs along the Sèves River just north of Périers. It was the site of a fierce battle on 26 July 1944 – the last before Périers was liberated the following day – which left the US 359th Regiment with 72 dead and 180 wounded. Two identical 2.3m-tall, granite stones are set at each end, where the path meets the road (northeast stone /// crammed.deadliest.banters; southwest stone /// giggly.biter.grounded).

Other memorials In Millières, a town 5km west, a waist-high rough granite stone has an inscription to pathfinders in the **US 8th Infantry Division** (in a layby on D431, 365m south of the D900 junction; /// tolerant.conjunction.stows), who liberated the town on 28 July, despite heavy opposition.

The **US 90th Infantry Division** are honoured with a memorial on the east bank of the Sèves River (at the end of a short footpath signposted from the Sèves road, nr Saint-Germain-sur-Sèves; /// roved.bran.undertones). It is a reminder of a strange story. On 23 July, the 358th Infantry Regiment, of the 90th Infantry Division, tried to assault the villages of Sèves and Saint-Germain-sur-Sèves on the high ground between marshes, called Sèves Island by the Americans. Losses were high on both sides, but worse for the Americans. In a field near this spot, a small unit of 44 German paratroopers (Fallschirmjäger) led by Staff Sergeant Alexander Uhlig managed to capture 244 US soldiers, including the battalion commander and his staff. Uhlig went to report to his commander, Major Friedrich von der Heydte, and

---

1 A memorial in Saint-Lô to Major Thomas D Howie of the US 29th Infantry Division. 2 US troops arriving in Saint-Lô, which had been heavily bombed, in August 1944. 3 The 90th Infantry Division 'Tough Ombres' monument in Périers. 4 The German war cemetery in Marigny. 5 The Bocage Breakout Museum in Saint-Martin-des-Besaces focuses on Allied efforts to advance through the region. ▶

ALASTAIR MCKENZIE

SS

ALASTAIR MCKENZIE

SS

MUSÉE LA PERCÉE DU BOCAGE

soon found himself having tea with his boss and some of the US officers he'd just captured. At 15.00, von der Heydte was told there were three US army chaplains carrying no weapons, just Red Cross flags, wandering by the river searching for wounded men. Impressed by their courage, von der Heydte agreed to a ceasefire so that the 100 US dead and 500 wounded could be moved.

HEADING SOUTH

Following the liberation of Saint-Lô, Allied forces began moving south from 25 July, as they launched Operation Cobra (see below), their bid to break free of the bocage and expand out of Normandy. There are plenty of worthwhile sights in the towns and villages on the route south, towards Vire and Falaise.

MARIGNY GERMAN WAR CEMETERY (Rue du Cimetière Allemand, Marigny-le-Lozon; 13km southwest of Saint-Lô; ⏱ 08.00–18.00 daily; free; ♿) Originally, two cemeteries – one German, one American – faced each other on either side of the road here. In the American cemetery were the graves of 3,070 troops who died during Operation Cobra. After the war they were reburied either in the American Cemetery at Colleville-sur-Mer (page 67) or the Brittany American Cemetery in Saint-James. Today, there are 11,169 German war graves, mostly from the Panzer Lehr Division, which suffered huge casualties on 25 July from air bombardments aiming to break the German lines between Saint-Lô and Périers. The soldiers are buried in pairs, with simple gravestones lying on the ground recording their names and dates.

General Erich Marcks, who commanded the 84th German Army Corps and was considered one of the best German generals in Normandy, is buried here. He was certainly one of the most prescient: he had always considered that the Allies might attack Normandy, not Pas-de-Calais, and in bad weather. When they did, he was one of the first German commanders to counter-attack. A few days later, on 12 June, he was on an inspection tour of his troops when a US fighter plane strafed his car. Marcks, who had had one leg amputated after being wounded in Ukraine in June

OPERATION COBRA

Launched on July 25, Operation Cobra was a pivotal moment in the Battle of Normandy. Orchestrated by Lieutenant General Omar Bradley, commander of the United States First Army, Cobra was a daring offensive aimed at shattering the heavily fortified German defences at the base of the Cotentin Peninsula and paving the way for a large-scale Allied advance.

The operation commenced with a huge aerial bombardment involving over 1,500 Allied bombers, who unleashed a relentless 'carpet of bombs' on the German frontline southwest of Saint-Lô, and, accidentally, some American positions too. It created a corridor for Allied ground troops to advance, under the protective cover of the aerial bombardment. American infantry and armoured units pushed through the weakened German lines.

The success of Operation Cobra had a far-reaching impact. It decisively shattered the stalemate that had gripped the battlefield for weeks, enabling Allied forces to regain momentum, driving German troops westward towards Brittany, while simultaneously turning east towards Le Mans. It thus set the stage for the encirclement and destruction of German forces at Falaise.

1941, was hit in his other leg by a 20mm cannon shell, and he quickly bled out and died. He is to be found here, sharing grave 1,478 with Private Gebhardt Eberhard.

The town of Marigny-le-Lozon is also where you can find the **Memorial Cobra Museum** (2 rue des Alleux; ℡ 02 33 56 04 47; w saintlo-tourisme.fr/annuaire-du-patrimoine/memorial-cobra; ⊕ Jun–Aug 14.30–18.30 Sat–Sun; free), a small museum with documents, a video, photos and objects from Operation Cobra (page 114).

SAINT-MARTIN-DES-BESACES AND AROUND This town, 30km south of Saint-Lô, is home to the **Bocage Breakout Museum** (Musée de La Percée du Bocage; 5 rue du 19 Mars 1962; ℡ 02 31 67 52 78; w laperceedubocage.fr; ⊕ hours & days vary, check website; adult/child €6/2), a relatively small but unusual museum focusing on the experiences of the British forces who fought their way through the bocage in Operation Bluecoat (page 116). The centrepiece of the museum, which is run by the enthusiastic and very knowledgeable Billy Lebond, is a large walk-around 3D map model illustrating the Battle for Saint-Martin-des-Besaces, liberated on 30 July by the British 11th Armoured Division.

Near Saint-Martin-des-Besaces, on a hill with a panoramic view, is the **Hill 309 memorial** (D53A, 2.6km east of Saint-Martin-des-Besaces; /// bickered.picket. soulmate). The dark grey stone commemorates the soldiers who died taking this hill on 30 July as part of Operation Bluecoat (page 116). The French monument names the soldiers but doesn't make mention of their company, the 4th Coldstream Guards. The unit's commander, Brigadier Sir Walter de Stopham Barttelot, is honoured at the nearby **Coldstream Hill memorial** (D675; /// grappling.decider.oppress). Barttelot, a key player in the battle to take the hill, died in combat shortly afterwards, on 16 August, and is buried in Saint-Charles-de-Percy CWGC cemetery (see below).

Near Les Loges village, 5km northeast of Saint-Martin-des-Besaces, is the **Hill 226 Scots Guards memorial** (Le Bourg/D292; /// culminated.constitutes. cornered). Two black marble stones record the taking of Hill 226, 6km behind enemy lines, on 30 July by the Scots Guards in their Churchill tanks. The Scots Guards achieved their main objective to take the hill, but they were intercepted there by three German Jagdpanther ('hunting panther') tank destroyers, which lived up to their name, destroying 11 tanks. Fresh infantry reinforcements were brought up to support what remained of the Scots Guards and on 1 August they fought off two German counter-attacks to secure the hill.

BULL BRIDGE (Pont du Taureau, Vaux de Souleuvre/D56, Souleuvre en Bocage; 120m south of the junction with D293; 30km southeast of Saint-Lô; /// keeps.filmy. salsa) Look closer at this seemingly insignificant bridge to discover a pair of small metal plaques with the image of a bull stamped on them. The bull is the emblem of the British 11th Armoured Division who were part of Operation Bluecoat (page 116). On 30 July, reconnaissance units of the 2nd Household Cavalry were astonished to find this bridge over the Souleuvre River intact and undefended. It turned out the bridge lay in a gap between two German divisions and there was a dispute about who should guard it. The British troops were quick to exploit the error: the 2nd Household Cavalry held the bridge for 2 hours before they were joined by tanks from the 2nd Northamptonshire Yeomanry, who then spearheaded the 11th Division's drive south.

SAINT-CHARLES-DE-PERCY CWGC CEMETERY (D290A, just south of the junction with D56; 35km southeast of Saint-Lô; ⅏) The southernmost CWGC cemetery

Operation Bluecoat (30 July–7 August 1944) was quickly planned by General Montgomery (page 26) to exploit German defences that had been weakened by Hitler's order to send the German 2nd Panzer Division west to try to cut off Operation Cobra (page 114), the American breakout at Avranches. It was a significant British offensive. The plan was to secure the vital road junction of Vire and the high ground of Mont-Pinçon, with the ultimate goal of breaking the stalemate in the Caen sector and opening up a path for further Allied advances.

The operation commenced with a heavy artillery bombardment, followed by coordinated assaults. VIII Corps of the British Second Army, led by Lieutenant General Oliver Leese, spearheaded the advance on the left flank, capturing the strategically important village of Buron and advancing towards Vire; meanwhile XXX Corps, commanded by Lieutenant General Horrocks, bore the brunt of German counter-attacks on the right flank, but managed to secure Mont-Pinçon, a crucial vantage point overlooking the battlefield.

British forces gradually pushed the Germans back and significantly weakened German defences in the Caen sector, paving the way for the wider Allied offensive to liberate Caen (page 124).

in Normandy, this site contains 809 graves: mainly British, plus two Australians and five Canadians. These soldiers were caught up in the major fighting between Caumont-l'Éventé and Vire as part of Operation Bluecoat (see above).

NOUES DE SIENNE You'll find a set of monuments in a small gravelled triangle in the village of Noues de Sienne (junction of D77 & D308; 42km south of Saint-Lô). Alongside a large, elaborate stone memorial to the **civilian victims** of both world wars, two granite headstones are dedicated to Allied units. The first is to the **US 2nd Armoured Division**, which is etched with their colourful 'Hell on Wheels' emblem, plus a Sherman tank underneath. The second, to **RAF Allied aircrew**, carries an image of a Wellington bomber and remembers airmen killed in three aircraft crashes nearby: two were in April 1941, but the third dates from the Battle of Normandy – when First Lieutenant Rudolph L Marko, from the USAAF 368th Fighter Group, crashed his P-47 Thunderbolt into a tree while strafing targets on 1 August 1944.

CORPORAL BATES MEMORIAL (Pavée, off D303; 43km southeast of Saint-Lô; /// smothered.purpose.delimit) Corporal Sidney Bates, of the Royal Norfolk Regiment, was in charge of a section near Sourdeval on 6 August. Attacked by the 10th SS Panzer Division, he seized a Bren gun from a dead comrade and charged. He was shot twice, but went on firing until wounded a third time. Bates, who was awarded the Victoria Cross, died in hospital two days later and is buried in Bayeux cemetery (page 64).

9

The Falaise Pocket and Gap

The area around Falaise was the scene, in August 1944, of the last major battle of the Normandy campaign. Allied forces encircled the remaining German troops in the so-called Falaise Pocket, a rapidly shrinking area between the Orne River to the west, Falaise to the north and Argentan to the south.

The beginning of the end had come on 1 August, when American forces broke through German lines at Avranches and began to race southwest across Brittany. The next day, against the advice of his generals, Hitler ordered most of his remaining tanks to be detached from fighting the British and Canadians around Caen, and sent them west to attack Mortain and Avranches, in a bid to cut off the American advance (the German attack on Mortain started on 7 August and didn't make it any further). Meanwhile, British, Canadian and Polish forces, having captured Caen, were steadily pushing south, while the Americans swung east towards Alençon, then north to Argentan. Seeing the danger of encirclement, the German 7th Army and 5th Panzer Army began rapidly retreating on 12 August. However, the hills and woods surrounding the Falaise Pocket gave the Allied forces cover for their troops, tanks and artillery, as well as panoramic views of the battlefield, while narrow roads and bridges made it difficult for the Germans to manoeuvre their forces.

On 19 August, the Allies closed the 'Gap' – the last remaining exit for the Germans, to the east, around Saint-Lambert-sur-Dives – when the US 15th Corps met the 2nd Canadian Corps at Chambois. Over the next few days, German forces

MORTAIN

The Battle for Mortain was one of the fiercest in Normandy. Over five days, 700 soldiers of the US 30th Infantry Division were besieged and isolated on Hill 314 overlooking the town. Short of ammunition and other supplies, they managed to hold out against numerous attacks by the German 17th SS Panzergrenadier Division. Rather belatedly, on 17 March 2020, President Donald J Trump announced that the 30th Infantry Division would be awarded the Presidential Unit Citation badge for exceptional heroism, in recognition of its stand at Mortain. The town falls outside the geographic scope of this guidebook, but if you wish to visit, there is a polished black stone stele dedicated to the **30th Division** (/// dryly.photograph.alerting) on Hill 314, and a spectacular **viewpoint** (/// mixing.sarong.pictured) from which 1st Lieutenant Charles A Barts and 2nd Lieutenant Robert L Weiss, of the 230th Field Artillery Battalion, were able to call down devastating artillery salvoes against the German forces as they tried to advance to Avranches.

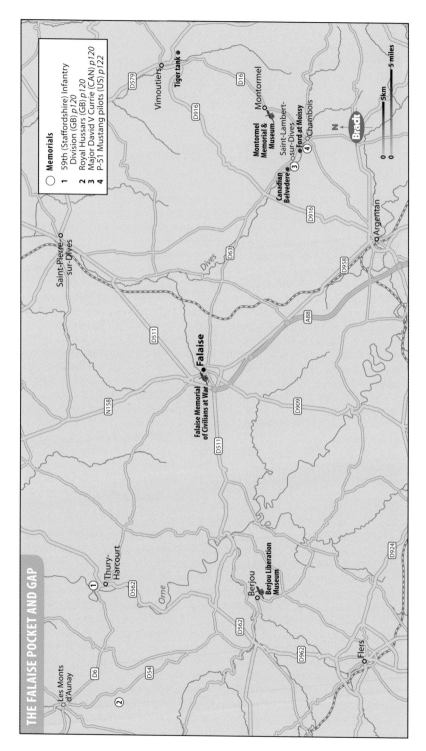

Memorials

1 59th (Staffordshire) Infantry
   Division (GB) *p120*
2 Royal Hussars (GB) *p120*
3 Major David V Currie (CAN) *p120*
4 P-51 Mustang pilots (US) *p122*

Vimoutiers

Tiger tank

Montormel

Montormel
Memorial &
Museum

Saint-Lambert-
sur-Dives

Canadian
Belvedere

Ford at Moissy

Chambois

N

Bradt

0   5km

0   5 miles

D579

D16

D916

D916

Argentan

Saint-Pierre-
sur-Dives

Dives

D63

D958

A88

D511

Falaise

Falaise Memorial
of Civilians at War

D511

N158

D909

Thury-
Harcourt

D562

Orne

Berjou

Berjou Liberation
Museum

Les Monts
d'Aunay

D6

D54

D562

D962

D924

Flers

were pounded by Allied artillery fire and bombing. By 22 August, the German 7th Army had been destroyed, and the severely weakened 5th Panzer Army began retreating to the German border. It has been estimated that approximately 20,000 Germans escaped, 10,000 were killed and 50,000 were taken prisoner during the action in the Falaise Gap. The Battle of the Falaise Pocket was a decisive victory for the Allies. It marked the end of the German army in Normandy and paved the way for the race to Paris and the liberation of France.

These days, as in 1944, wooded hills look down on to the Falaise Pocket. It's a peaceful part of Normandy, with empty back roads and quiet villages, and much less hustle and bustle than the coast and its towns.

FALAISE

Falaise is inextricably linked with William the Conqueror, who was born in the heavily restored château that dominates the town from its rocky outcrop. Cobbled streets, medieval stone ramparts and a church dating from the days of William give the impression of a genuine old quarter, but two-thirds of the town was destroyed during World War II and what you see is mainly the result of careful restoration.

The **tourist information office** is by the Falaise Memorial of Civilians in War (5 pl Guillaume le Conquérant; 02 31 90 17 26; w falaise-suissenormande.com; year-round, hours vary but often 09.30–12.30 & 13.30–17.30; check website).

GETTING THERE AND AROUND If **driving**, Falaise lies 38km south of Caen on the N158 and can be reached from all the **ferry** ports by leaving the A13/N13 at Caen (page 124). By **train**, you'll need to disembark at Caen, and then take a bus onwards or drive. By **bus**, Nomad line 118 will take you from Caen to Falaise (w nomad.normandie.fr/lignes-de-cars/ligne-118; runs daily, check timetable online; 1hr 14mins).

Falaise is easy to **walk** or **cycle** around, but to get to the other sites in this chapter, you will need a car or to take a **tour**.

WHAT TO SEE AND DO
Falaise Memorial of Civilians in War (Le Mémorial de Falaise des Civils dans La Guerre, 12 pl Guillaume le Conquérant; 02 31 06 06 45; w memorial-falaise. com; days & hours vary, check website; adult/10–18yrs/under-10s €8.50/6/free) The Falaise Memorial, in a modern building on the remains of an old bombed-out mansion, commemorates the civilians caught up in World War II (over 400,000 killed in France) with a moving series of testimonies, photos and personal objects. The total number of civilians killed in all regions of the war was 40 million, while more than 30 million people were displaced. The memorial also brings the experience of citizens in Normandy to life through videos in English and French.

WEST OF FALAISE

BERJOU LIBERATION MUSEUM (Musée de la Libération de Berjou Les Cours, 26.5km from Falaise; m 06 71 82 24 96; w musee-berjou.fr; year-round 14.00–18.00 Sun; free) This museum (also called Blackwater 39/45 Museum) focuses on the fighting in 15–17 August 1944 around the Noireau River, one of the last battles before the Falaise Gap was closed. It's a small museum displaying uniforms, small arms, bits of equipment and personal items found on the battlefield.

MEMORIALS A low stone wall in the village of Le Hom honours those who died serving with the British **59th (Staffordshire) Infantry Division** (junction of D6 & D562, 28km northwest of Falaise). The 59th was short-lived. Only formed in 1939, it spent five years training before being the last British division assigned to Operation Overlord, arriving in Normandy in early July. The men first faced the enemy during Operation Charnwood (page 126), and five weeks later, in their final battle during 9 to 14 August, they fought their way across the Orne River near Thury-Harcourt. However, after the last battle in the Falaise Pocket, as the most junior division, they were disbanded and re-allocated to units that had suffered heavy casualties.

Mont-Pinçon, 365m above sea level, is one of the highest points in Normandy – and here you'll find the **Royal Hussars monument** (6.4km south of Les Monts d'Aunay off D54; signposted up an unpaved road opposite the Mont-Pinçon transmitter station; /// bustled.headrests.helpers). The British 13th/18th Royal Hussars played a vital role in capturing Mont-Pinçon on 5–7 August, a tactically important victory that enabled the Allies to advance safely towards the Falaise Pocket. It also knocked out a radio direction finder beam which had guided the Luftwaffe towards targets in England. A plaque has a map of the battlefield and an inscription that describes 'the qualities which [the battle] called forth in the men concerned'.

EAST OF FALAISE

SAINT-LAMBERT-SUR-DIVES (23km southeast of Falaise) In 1944, the village of Saint-Lambert-sur-Dives was a scene of fierce and chaotic fighting, right at the heart of the final defeat of the Germans in Normandy. Today it is a quiet village of small stone houses in the middle of rolling farmland. It was captured on 21 August by the 4th Canadian Armoured Division, and a viewpoint overlooking the village and nearby Chambois – where the final battle to close the Falaise Gap was fought – is topped with a **Canadian Belvedere** (D13, 750m north of Saint-Lambert-sur-Dives centre; /// bargained.procreation.lash). Built by the Canadian Battlefield Foundation, it is well worth visiting for the views and good maps that explain what you are looking at. Just south of the belvedere is a memorial to **Major David V Currie** (junction of Le Bourg & D13), of Canada's South Alberta Regiment. Currie was awarded the Commonwealth's highest award, the Victoria Cross, for his 'gallant leadership' of a small force of Canadian tanks, anti-tank guns and 130 infantry soldiers in the three-day Battle for Saint-Lambert-sur-Dives. The bronze plaque details his actions, which resulted in 300 Germans killed, 500 wounded and an astonishing 2,100 taken prisoner.

GOUFFERN EN AUGE The peaceful little **ford at Moissy** (Gué de Moissy, on the unpaved La Doitière road off D13 north of Gouffern en Auge village; /// placated. manhole.sneezed) is one of the most evocative sites in Normandy. Today it's nestled among the trees and has a little picnic table; around 19 August 1944, it was a scene of bloody carnage and panic as the remnants of the German army sought to escape through the Falaise Gap. Vehicles and equipment were abandoned and Germans

---

1 The Montormel Memorial sits on top of Hill 262. 2 The Royal Hussars memorial on Mont-Pinçon. 3 The German tiger tank at Vimoutiers. 4 The ford at Moissy, where German troops tried to flee the Falaise Pocket. 5 A gas mask on display at the Falaise Memorial museum, which focuses on civilian experiences during World War II. ▶

ANDIA/A

ALASTAIR MCKENZIE

MARIANNE ROED JENSEN/D

ALASTAIR MCKENZIE

JULIEN JEAN/D

fought each other as they frantically tried to get across one of the last crossing points of the Dives River, while Allied aircraft and artillery bombarded them. It became known as the 'corridor of death'. It is one of the points of interest on the 'August 44' self-driving route (see opposite).

Just 270m south of the ford you'll find a simple and sad **memorial to two P-51 Mustang pilots** (/// disappoint.remorse.misfortunes). On the morning of 13 August, 2nd Lieutenant Chester H Rice and 1st Lieutenant Dell P Hudson, of the USAAF 382nd Fighter Squadron, were strafing the fleeing Germans as they tried to cross the ford at Moissy. It is believed that either the sun or dust and smoke from below momentarily blinded them and they collided. Hudson's body was never found.

MONTORMEL MEMORIAL AND MUSEUM (Les Hayettes, Mont-Ormel; 29km southeast of Falaise; 02 33 67 38 61; w memorial-montormel.fr; Apr & Sep–Oct 10.00–17.00 daily; May–Aug 09.30–18.00 daily; Nov–Mar 10.00–17.30 Sat–Mon; adult/child €6/2.50) As German forces were trying to flee the Falaise Pocket, the 1st Polish Armoured Division, led by Major General Stanisław Maczek and attached to Canadian forces, captured Hill 240 outside Écorches and Hill 262 at Montormel on 19 August. The Germans threw everything they had at the Poles in an effort to reopen the Gap. With artillery support from the Canadians, the Poles managed to hold on to their position – but not without heavy losses: when they had arrived on Hill 262, they comprised 2,000 men, 60 officers and 87 tanks; when they were relieved on 21 August, they were down to 30 tanks, less than 100 men, and just four officers.

The Montormel Memorial, built on the summit of Hill 262 and opened in 1965, features a large stone wall with an archway and a terrace, which has panoramic views across the Falaise–Argentan battleground. There is a large orientation map, an M8 light armoured car in the colours of General Charles de Gaulle's Free French (page 63), and an M4A1 Sherman tank with General Maczek's name painted on it. This tank didn't fight at Montormel, but it did come from the 1st Polish Armoured Division. In the woods to the north there is a bust of **General Maczek** on a pedestal (/// offer.foresee.grazes). The museum, which is built into the side of the hill by the terrace and is grassed over to minimise its visual impact, displays artefacts and images from the fighting. It also airs a documentary every 15 minutes about the battle, and when it ends, the wall opposite opens like a vertical blind to let the audience look out to the panoramic bay window, which has signage and photos illustrating where the events took place on the landscape in front.

TIGER TANK (Char Tigre, La Butte du Sap lay-by off D979, 1km southeast of Vimoutiers; /// attributing.trifle.vibrate) This tank may look insignificant, but it's a well-known historic monument. Panzerkampfwagen VI Tiger Ausf E No 251, to give it its full name, was one of the few tanks that escaped the Falaise Gap. It was probably heading for a fuel dump in Ticheville, only 5km away, when it ran out of fuel and was abandoned by its crew, who set two charges to disable it before they left. The Canadian army, in hot pursuit, pushed the Tiger off the road and into a ditch, where it lay until 1975, when the local commune bought it and mounted it on a concrete plinth close to where it was originally abandoned. It was registered as a historic monument that same year. There is a plan to move the tank down into the town (which also has an excellent Camembert Museum), and create a museum there.

The August 44 circuit is a self-drive tour (around 30km) of ten key locations in the Falaise Pocket. At each point there are boards explaining what happened on that spot, with before and after photos. The sights include Saint-Lambert-sur-Dives (page 120), the ford at Moissy (page 120), and Hill 262 and the Montormel Memorial (see opposite).

10

Caen and Around

The large city of Caen, capital of Calvados, traces its historic importance back to the 11th century and William the Conqueror. His formidable castle, which now houses two museums – the Museum of Normandy and the Fine Art Museum of Normandy – stands at the centre of the old quarter. William and his Flemish wife Matilda also built the two magnificent abbeys: the Abbaye aux Hommes and the Abbaye aux Dames.

For the Allies, particularly the British and Commonwealth forces who landed on the two easternmost beaches, Sword and Juno, Caen was the great objective. D-Day may have come as a massive surprise to the Germans, but they weren't slow to react, and whether or not the plan to capture Caen in 24 to 48 hours was realistically achievable, its capture remained the great objective for much of the Battle of Normandy.

Tragically, between June and late July 1944, Caen suffered some of the most destructive bombing of World War II, followed by fierce fighting. The conflict reduced this once-magnificent city to crumbling ruins: 80% of the city was destroyed and 3,000 citizens killed. Thankfully, when you walk through the old streets today, you'll find it hard to distinguish what is genuinely old and what has been rebuilt. The restoration of much of the city has been done in Caen stone (the same stone used by William the Conqueror to build the Tower of London), and it took from 1948 to 1962 to complete the restoration work, which included the castle. Fortunately, neither of the two grand abbeys were badly bombed.

While Caen was being reduced to rubble, most of the battles to capture it were being fought out around the edges, particularly around the eastern and then southern outskirts. Caen was the lynchpin. Until it was taken nobody could advance south towards Falaise or east towards the Seine. All this explains why there are only a few sites of interest in the city itself, but a profusion of memorials and cemeteries in the region around Caen.

CAEN

GETTING THERE AND AROUND By **air**, Air France (w airfrance.co.uk) flies to Caen from major French cities, as well as some European destinations, but it will

CAEN

○ **Memorials**
1 59th (Staffordshire) Infantry Division (GB) *p127*
2 Cambes-en-Plaine memorial *p127*
3 Royal Ulster Rifles (GB) *p127*
4 Norwegian memorial *p127*
5 9th Infantry Brigade (CAN) *p127*
6 1st Battalion, Queen's Own Rifles (CAN) *p127*
7 Abbaye d'Ardenne Canadian Massacre *p129*
8 North Nova Scotia Highlanders (CAN) *p129*
9 Highland Light Infantry & Sherbrooke Fusiliers (CAN) *p129*
10 Royal Winnipeg Rifles (CAN) *p130*
11 Nottinghamshire (Sherwood Rangers) Yeomanry (GB) *p130*
12 49th West Riding Division (GB) *p131*
13 Jerusalem crossroads *p131*
14 Typhoon pilots *p132*
15 George Rarey *p132*
16 Hill 112 *p132*
17 Point 67 (CAN) *p133*
18 2nd Battalion, Royal Lincolnshire Regiment (GB) *p134*

usually be easier to fly to Paris and take a train or bus. Caen lies on the main A13/N13 road, so by **car** it is easily reached from the **ferry** ports (page 5) or the **Channel Tunnel** (page 5). To drive from Paris, you'll also take the A13 (246km; 2hrs 50mins; tolls approx €18), or from Cherbourg take the N13 (122km; 1hr 30mins). There are regular direct **trains** from Paris Saint-Lazare (2hrs 17mins) and Cherbourg (1hr 10mins). By **bus** from Paris, take FlixBus or BlaBlaCar Bus (page 7), taking from 2hrs 40mins. There are bus services between Caen and the landing beaches, but these are few and far between and only operate for certain months, days and times (see individual beach chapters for more information). Within the city, including getting from the train station, take a **tram** (number T1, T2 or T3; w twisto.fr/reseau-twisto/nos-mobilites/reseau-tramway). To get to the surrounding sites, you can try the buses (good luck!), drive or take a **tour**.

TOURIST INFORMATION

Tourist office 12 pl Saint-Pierre; ℡ 02 31 27 14 14; w caenlamer-tourisme.com; ⏱ Apr–Jun & Sep 09.30–18.30 Mon & Wed–Sat, 10.00–18.30 Tue; 09.30–13.30 Sun & bank hols; Jul–Aug

09.00–19.00 Mon–Sat, 10.00-13.00 & 14.00-19.00 Sun & public hols; Oct–Mar 09.30–13.00 & 14.00–18.00 Mon & Wed–Sat, 11.00–13.00 & 14.00–18.00 Tue

WHAT TO SEE AND DO

Caen Memorial Museum (Mémorial de Caen, esp Général Eisenhower; ℡ 02 31 06 06 44; w normandy.memorial-caen.com; ⏱ 2–6 Jan, 30 Jan–Mar & Oct 09.00–18.00 daily; Apr–Sep 09.00–19.00 daily; Nov–Dec 09.30–18.00 Thu–Tue; also closed 6 Jun & 25 Dec; adult/child 10–18yrs/under-10s €19.80/17.50/free;

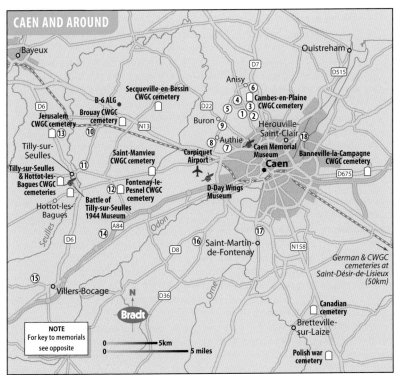

On D-Day, the objective of the British 3rd Infantry Division was to seize Caen, or at least to reach its suburbs, while the Canadian 3rd Infantry Division was to cut the Caen–Bayeux road and capture Carpiquet Airport just to the west. The day went well, even if progress was slow. But then, on 7 June, they ran into the 12th SS Panzer Division 'Hitlerjugend' (Hitler Youth), who ruthlessly counter-attacked. There was fierce fighting around the villages and communes of Anisy, Cambes-en-Plaine, Galmanche, Saint-Contest, Buron and Authie. In some places the Allies were pushed back; in others, they held, but they did not reach Caen. That would take a succession of carefully planned operations:

- **Operation Perch** (7–14 June): An attempt to outflank the Germans southwest of Caen through Tilly-sur-Seulles and Villers-Bocage, where the Allies were halted and driven back.
- **Operation Epsom** (26–30 June): An offensive intended to sweep around closer to Caen than Perch, cross the Odon River, take Hill 112 and cross the Orne River to reach Bretteville-sur-Laize to the south of Caen. The Allies got across the Odon and reached Hill 112 but were pushed back to the river.
- **Operation Charnwood** (8–12 July): No more sweeping around the outside. The main thrust of Charnwood was into Caen from the north, preceded by a heavy bombing raid, and from the west through Carpiquet. By noon on 9 July, the Canadians and British had captured the northwest half of the city up to the Orne River. Meanwhile…
- **Operation Jupiter** (10–11 July): This was designed to firm up the ground taken on the east bank of the Odon and re-capture Hill 112. It managed the first objective but not the second.
- **Operation Goodwood** (18–20 July): This time the approach was from the east. Three British armoured divisions moved around the east side of Caen and south towards the high ground on the east bank of the Orne River around Bourguébus. With the pincer movement of operations Goodwood and Atlantic (below), Caen was captured, but the attempts to move further south were repelled.
- **Operation Atlantic** (18–21 July): The Canadian 2nd Corps took the remaining half of Caen and pressed down into the Orne Valley.

Caen memorial app) The Caen Memorial, which covers both world wars, is one of the best introductions to those devastating conflicts and it's large enough to cover aspects that often get glossed over elsewhere, including the difficult issue of enemy collaboration. It has an impressive number of artefacts and some excellent films; it is particularly good on the D-Day landings and the Battle of Normandy, including the liberation of Caen, Operation Cobra (page 114) and the Falaise Pocket.

Don't miss **German General Wilhelm Richter's HQ** in tunnels underneath the museum. Richter commanded the 716th Static Infantry Division responsible for the Atlantic Wall defences. It was not a lucky assignment. There is an account of a conversation between him and one of his officers as he evacuated his HQ at 16.00 on D-Day. He was completely overwhelmed and disoriented, with tears streaming down his face. When asked what they should do and where the enemy were, he simply didn't know. Within a fortnight of D-Day, most of his division was killed, captured or wounded. Richter lost command of his division and was sent to command a division in occupied Norway. He saw no more active combat and survived the war.

NORTH OF CAEN

CAMBES-EN-PLAINE Near this village, 6km north of Caen, the British **59th (Staffordshire) Infantry Division**, who had arrived in Normandy on 27 June, first faced battle during Operation Charnwood (see opposite). Early on 8 July, the 59th encountered elements of the Hitlerjugend Division in a trench system between Cambes-en-Plaine and the village of La Bijude, and defeated them. Yet, when the front moved on, the surviving Hitler Youth reoccupied the trenches, and the 59th had to retake them later in the day. A low stone stele among the trees commemorates the troops and the action here (unmarked road west of D79; /// power.smelter.potato). There is also a small memorial plaque to the 59th on the wall of the churchyard at nearby Saint-Contest, and another further south at Le Hom (page 120).

In the centre of the village, which was captured by units of the 59th Division and the 3rd Infantry Division on 9 June before their advance was hampered, there is a **liberation memorial** (junction of D79B, rue du Colombier & rue des Prés), a simple white headstone with stone angel wings carved with the two divisions' emblems. There is also a small **CWGC cemetery** (rue de Mesnil Ricard; ♿), on a quiet road on the northern outskirts of the village. Of the 224 graves, over half were from the 59th Division; many of the burials date from the Charnwood Operation of 8 to 12 July.

By the cemetery is a memorial to the **Royal Ulster Rifles** (cnr of D220A & rue du Mesnil Ricard); the dates on the plaque run from 6 June to 16 September 1944, in memory of 'all ranks of the 2nd Battalion of the Royal Ulster Rifles' who helped liberate Cambes-en-Plaine and lost their lives in subsequent fighting.

OTHER MEMORIALS Between Cambes-en-Plaine and the village of Villons-les-Buissons, which lies 3.5km west, you'll find the **Norwegian memorial** (junction of rue des Cambes & D79), a tall pink stone pillar standing out among flat fields. A metal relief image shows aeroplanes, ships, and soldiers running on a beach, below which a plaque in French and Norwegian commemorates 'with the greatest respect' the 52 Norwegians killed on D-Day, and the 3,000 Norwegian soldiers, sailors and airmen who fought with the Allies in World War II.

Continuing to Villons-les-Buissons, a memorial to the **9th Canadian Brigade** (cnr of rue des Glengarrians & D220), lists the names of those who died from 7 to 10 June in this place. When the Canadian advance on Caen was stopped by the Hitlerjugend Division, the front line was drawn here. The 9th Brigade dug in and resisted German counter-attacks for a month, until the launch of Operation Charnwood on 8 July. During this time it became known as 'Hell's Corner'.

On D-Day, the Canadian **1st Battalion, Queen's Own Rifles** landed on Juno Beach, captured Bernières-sur-Mer with the Fort Garry Horse Regiment (page 36), then fought its way to the village of Anisy, 8km north of Caen, reaching it in the evening. Of all the Canadian regiments, the Queen's Own Rifles suffered the highest casualties: 143 were killed, wounded or captured. To commemorate them, two cream-coloured stones stand side by side with a maple leaf cut out (D220 in Anisy, just east of the junction with rue du Clos Saint-Pierre; /// yelps.automating. coped). A small plaque honours 'those gallant members… who gave their lives to take, and hold, Anisy'.

WEST OF CAEN

ABBAYE D'ARDENNE CANADIAN MASSACRE MEMORIAL (L'Abbaye D'Ardenne, rue d'Ardennes, Authie, 4km northwest of Caen; `02 31 29 37 37; w veterans. gc.ca; search 'Abbaye D'Ardenne'; ⊕ 14.00–18.00 Tue–Fri; free; &) In a short passageway beside the magnificent abbey, a large metal plaque relates the brutal story here. Members of the Hitlerjugend Division watched from their viewpoint in the tower as Canadian troops from the North Nova Scotia Highlanders and the 27th Armoured Regiment approached. In the Battle for Authie that followed on 7 June, 18 Canadians were captured, brought here and murdered. Two more died on 17 June. When the abbey was liberated on 8 July, one body was discovered; the others were found in 1945. They had been shot or bludgeoned to death. In a small garden at the end of the path, photos of each soldier hang on the walls, while panels recount their personal details and how their bodies were discovered. Canadian flags are tied around the trees and there's a little memorial and tributes left by relatives. The simplicity of the garden beside the very grand abbey adds a real poignancy to the history. The soldiers' remains are buried in the cemeteries at Bény-sur-Mer (page 44), Bretteville-sur-Laize (page 133), and one, private Hollis L McKiel, in Ryes (page 53).

In total, up to 156 Canadian prisoners of war are believed to have been murdered during the Battle of Normandy. Kurt Meyer, Commander of the 25th Panzergrenadier Regiment (of the Hitlerjugend Division), was tried for war crimes and was imprisoned until 1954.

In Authie town square, a simple stone monument pays tribute to the **North Nova Scotia Highlanders** (pl des Canadiens). Here, 84 soldiers and seven citizens lost their lives on 7 June.

BURON On 7 June 1944, the village of Buron (4.5km northwest of Caen) was briefly occupied by units of the Canadian 3rd Division, before being ejected by the Hitlerjugend Division. It wasn't until the start of Operation Charnwood a month later, on 8 July, that the village was re-taken by Canada's **Highland Light Infantry and Sherbrooke Fusiliers**, supported by the British Royal Artillery (RA). The Battle for Buron was fierce and bloody: the HLI suffered 262 casualties, of which 62 were fatal; the Sherbrooke tank squadron lost 11 of its 15 tanks; and the British 245th anti-tank battery lost four Achilles tanks, with a further four damaged. The village square has two stone memorials, to the Highland Light Infantry and the 27th Armoured Regiment of the Sherbrooke Fusiliers (pl des Canadiens).

D-DAY WINGS MUSEUM (485 rue Jules Védrines, Bretteville-sur-Odon, 7km west of Caen; m 06 72 42 60 52; w ddaywingsmuseum.com; ⊕ 09.30–18.30 daily; adult/ ages 7–16/under-16s €9/6/free) This museum is housed in a large hangar on the edge of Carpiquet Airport, which was so important to both the Allies and Germans in June 1944. Inside there are some interesting and authentic pieces of equipment, such as an anti-aircraft gun and searchlight, a B-17 Flying Fortress's gun turret and a Beechcraft C-45 light transport aircraft. You can try putting on a parachute, and there's also a collection of USAAF flying jackets.

◀ 1 Caen Memorial Museum offers a thought-provoking overview of both world wars. 2 A memorial to the Canadian Queen's Own Rifles in Anisy. 3 Urville is home to the only Polish war cemetery in France. 4 German troops surrender at Saint-Lambert-sur-Dives on 21 August 1944.

B-6 ALG (Junction of chem de l'Ancien Presbytere & rte de Coulombs, Thue et Mue; 4.5km northeast of Brouay CWGC cemetery; see opposite) A rough-hewn granite stele beside the road, in front of a semi-circular hedge, marks the site of this advanced landing ground. One plaque has a stylish etching of a typhoon and the dates when this advanced landing ground (page 125), built by the British Royal Engineers, was used: 16 June to 30 August; a second is a memorial to the 234 Squadron (Typhoons) and their acting squadron leader, Christopher 'Kit' North-Lewis. Decorated many times, one of his citations praises his 'skilful leadership, great tactical ability and iron determination'.

ROYAL WINNIPEG RIFLES MEMORIAL (In the car park opposite the town hall on rue du Moutier, Audrieu) A section of an old stone wall has been framed with stone pillars. On it are bronze plaques remembering 58 Canadian Royal Winnipeg Rifles soldiers, as well as eight soldiers from supporting units, who were captured and later shot by units of the Hitlerjugend Division between 8 and 11 June in three nearby locations: Le Mesnil-Patry, Le Haut du Bosq and Château d'Audrieu barely 300 metres away. Another small black bronze plaque remembers two British soldiers from the Durham Light Infantry who were also shot at Château d'Audrieu. The Juno Beach Centre (page 41) records that in these incidents and others, such as the massacre at Abbaye d'Ardenne (page 129), a total of 156 Canadians were murdered by the German SS. One out of every seven Canadians killed in Normandy from 6 to 11 June was not killed in combat but was executed as a POW.

TILLY-SUR-SEULLES AND AROUND This town, 23km west of Caen, was taken and retaken 23 times from 7 to 19 June 1944, was almost completely destroyed and lost a tenth of its population. It was not a strategic target, it just happened to be caught up in the fight for the countryside between Bayeux and Caen. Fighting continued around the town until mid-July. The **Battle of Tilly-sur-Seulles 1944 Museum** (rue du 18 Juin 1944; ☏02 31 80 92 10; w tilly1944.com/musee; ⏱ May–Sep 10.00–12.30 & 14.00–18.00 Sat–Sun; year-round by appointment for groups; adult/12–18/under-12 €4/2/free), housed in a former chapel, tells the town's story very effectively with large panels of photos and text in French and English.

A memorial to the British **Nottinghamshire (Sherwood Rangers) Yeomanry** sits 1.5km northeast of the town centre (rte d'Andrieu/D82; /// tropics.smarter. historically; ♿). On 11 June, the Sherwood Rangers HQ in nearby Saint-Pierre was shelled, killing the acting Colonel Major M H Laycock, Captain G A Jones and intelligence officer Lieutenant A Head. The officers are commemorated with a small brass plaque. They are buried in **Tilly-sur-Seulles CWGC cemetery** (D13, 1km west of the town; ♿), which is a peaceful spot: mature trees surround the cemetery on three sides and rose bushes climb the pergolas beside the rows of graves of 990 Commonwealth soldiers and 232 Germans. The war poet Keith Douglas, serving in the Sherwood Rangers Yeomanry, was killed on 9 June and buried by the chaplain near where he died, but was reburied here after the war. The majority of the dead here came from the fierce fighting in June and July in the push to Caen.

In a sign of how fierce the fighting was, there are another three CWGC cemeteries within 7km of the one at Tilly-sur-Seulles with graves of soldiers mostly killed in that campaign. At **Hottot-les-Bagues CWGC cemetery** (D9, just west of D6 junction; 2km south of Tilly-sur-Seulles; ♿ with help up small steps), where wisteria growing over the pergolas adds vivid colour in the summer, there are 965 Commonwealth graves. Among these lie three Australians, two New Zealanders, one South African and 34 Canadians, including Brigadier James Hargest, a much-decorated soldier who was about to change roles – he was leaving the British 50th Division, which he had commanded, to take on the job of repatriating released New Zealand prisoners of war – when he was killed by shellfire. Some 56 graves are unidentified, while the 24 soldiers of the Scots Guards (3rd Tank Battalion) buried here mostly died on Hill 226 (page 115). Also here are 32 German graves, their stones inscribed just with the soldier's name and dates, or '*Ein Deutscher Soldat*' ('a German soldier') for the unknown; but here they are standing stones, unlike in German cemeteries where the stones lie flat on the ground.

Fontenay-le-Pesnel CWGC cemetery (off D139, just north of junction with D173A; 1.8km east of Tessel; ♿) is a peaceful spot surrounded by uninterrupted farmland views; it feels as if it is in the middle of nowhere. The 460 Commonwealth graves come mainly from the South Staffordshire, East Lancashire and Royal Warwickshire regiments and the Durham Light Infantry, while there are 59 German graves. At the side of the track leading to the cemetery, where it meets the D139, you can't miss the impressive memorial to the **49th West Riding Division**. It features a cross with a rectangular stone beneath inscribed with the division's name and their roaring polar bear insignia, while stones dedicated to individual battalions are set in the wall behind the cross. The memorial was the idea of the division itself as a way of commemorating so many soldiers who served, and died, in the battles around Caen and who are buried in the surrounding cemeteries.

Jerusalem CWGC cemetery (D6, just north of junction with D187; 5.3km north of Tilly-sur-Seulles; ♿) is one of the smallest CWGC cemeteries in Normandy, surrounded by farmland and sheltered from the road by bushes. It holds just 46 Commonwealth war graves, one Czech grave and one unknown British grave, arranged in a semi-circle of three rows. The soldiers had been fighting in Tilly-sur-Seulles on 9 June against a German armoured column that tried to retake Bayeux. Just north of the cemetery is the **Jerusalem crossroads memorial** (junction of D6 & D33). On this spot, the British Inns of Court Regiment were caught up in bombing by an American P-47 Thunderbolt. It blew up their Royal Engineers' half-track, which was carrying explosives for the demolition of the bridges over the Orne River south of Caen. The small stone remembers the six soldiers and five civilians who were killed.

OTHER CWGC CEMETERIES

Saint-Manvieu (D9, just west of junction with D83; 10km west of Caen; ♿) One of the larger war cemeteries, Saint-Manvieu is an impressive place, with two pillars at the entrance and a large sandstone building containing the register of the dead, behind a rectangular stone etched with the words 'Their Name Liveth for Evermore'. This is another cemetery where the 1,627 Commonwealth burials came from the June to July offensive between Caen and Tilly-sur-Seulles (see opposite). Of these, 49 are unidentified. There are also 555 German graves.

Secqueville-en-Bessin (Off D126, 12km northwest of Caen; ♿) This small cemetery is tucked away in open farmland down an unpaved road; flat fields stretch away into the distance. The troops buried here were killed in the advance towards Caen in July 1944. There are 99 Commonwealth graves in three rows beside the stone cross, while 18 German graves are to the right of the entrance. Unlike many cemeteries, this one is not strictly symmetrical and you get a feeling for what it might have looked like during the war itself.

Brouay (Thue et Mue, next to the church; 15km northwest of Caen) This dedicated grassed slope at the top of the main churchyard cemetery is a pretty spot with a bench surrounded by wild rose bushes. There are 375 British and two Canadian graves, most of whom died in the heavy fighting around Caen in June and July. It's a peaceful spot to reflect on the battles as you take in the panoramic view over the valley to the southwest.

SOUTH OF CAEN

TYPHOON PILOTS MEMORIAL (At the junction of D83 & D675, Noyers-Bocage) A dramatic 3.5m-high black marble monument, shaped as two arrows meeting, with an etching underneath of a Hawker Typhoon in flight, commemorates the 151 Typhoon pilots killed in Normandy between May and August 1944. To one side a black marble plaque, with etchings of a Typhoon in flight and another on the ground being serviced, is 'dedicated to the glorious memory of all Typhoon pilots and supporting staff who gave their lives in World War II'.

GEORGE RAREY STELE (Junction of rte de Caumont and D67, Villers-Bocage; /// scholarships.traitor.left) Captain George Rarey, a popular pilot with the 379th Fighter Squadron (P-47 Thunderbolts), was also a cartoonist and commercial artist who painted nose art on up to 30 aircraft in his squadron. He is honoured here with an unusual rough-granite memorial on which, above the formal bronze plaque recording that he died (hit by flak) near this spot on 27 June, is a cartoon of him etched on a copper plate, smoking a pipe and with a pencil tucked behind his ear. George – nicknamed 'Dad' by his comrades due to his age (yet he was still only 27) – drew both funny and serious images of life as a pilot in sketchbooks and on postcards.

HILL 112 MEMORIAL (Off D8 between Éterville & Évrecy; /// citizen.playfulness. winning; ⊕ daily; free; ♿) Hardly a defined peak, Hill 112 is more a rolling plateau, with panoramic views over the surrounding countryside. This, and its location southwest of Caen between the Odon and Orne rivers, made it strategically important to hold for the Germans, and critically vital to capture for the Allies. German leader Erwin Rommel had recognised its significance well before the invasion and said: 'The side that controls Hill 112 will be the side that controls Lower Normandy.'

In the closing stages of Operation Epsom (page 126), the 15th Scottish Division managed to get across the Odon at Tourville and, with the 11th Armoured Division, fought their way to the top of Hill 112. However, the salient they had created was narrow, and newly arriving Panzer divisions were pressing on three sides. The British had to withdraw. It took a month of fierce fighting before the Germans finally abandoned their positions on 4 August, not because of the assault but to respond to the American breakout in the west (Operation Cobra; page 114).

According to the Hill 112 Memorial Foundation (w thehill112.com), who are responsible for the memorial park at the top of the plateau, this fighting cost the lives of 10,000 German and Allied soldiers. The 43rd (Wessex) Infantry Division suffered 7,000 casualties between 10 and 22 July. The park includes several monuments, including a 2m-tall stone obelisk, dedicated to the **43rd (Wessex) Infantry Division**. Erected shortly after the war ended it was, surprisingly, carved by German stonemasons in the town of Uelzen near Belsen; apparently they were nervous about visiting France so soon after the war.

Nearby is a large mound with a knee-height marble plinth featuring an orientation map (now a little faded) and the emblems of some of the regiments who fought on the hill. Three have been blanked out: they were of SS units, but it is illegal to display Nazi emblems in Normandy and, after protests, they were removed. At the edges of the mound, 19 short stone pillars name local villages and communes that contributed to the funding of the memorial, with arrows etched on them to indicate where they are. Some have numbers indicating how many of their citizens were killed in the war. Next to the mound, a **Mk VII Churchill tank** commemorates the tank crews who fought on Hill 112 and in the surrounding villages.

Between the mound and the main road, a large gravel area in the shape of a **Maltese cross** is marked out with 112 commemorative trees. At the centre of the cross, a life-size bronze statue of a British infantryman advancing with rifle and bayonet honours the infantry who died in the battle for Hill 112. In one of the four quarters of the cross is a **25-pounder field gun** commemorating the role of the Royal Artillery in 1944. This area, with the trees, statue and field gun, was unveiled by HRH Prince Edward in July 2017.

POINT 67 CANADIAN MEMORIAL (North of Saint-Martin-de-Fontenay on D562A; 7km south of Caen; /// relaxing.lifters.powers; ⊕ 09.00–19.00 daily; free)

In Operation Atlantic of 18–21 July (page 126), the 2nd Canadian Corps cleared the industrial suburbs of Caen and captured Point 67 (sometimes called Hill 67), the first of a series of battles pushing the Germans south towards Falaise. Point 67 is now a major Canadian site, with views over the Orne River valley to the west. Its plaques and memorials honour all those Canadian units who took part in Operation Atlantic and subsequent battles. Among them were the Calgary Highlanders who, to the sound of bagpipes, took this position on the evening of 19 July, supported by artillery fire from the 5th Canadian Field Artillery Regiment and the tanks of the Sherbrooke Fusiliers. Another board explains how the Black Watch (Royal Highland Regiment) suffered 307 casualties on 25 July at the hands of the 2nd SS Panzer Division as they tried to move 4km south along the ridge to Fontenay-le-Marmion. A nearby 25-pounder field gun acts as a memorial to 'all Canadian gunners who served in the Normandy Campaign and to the 463 members of the Royal Regiment of Canadian Artillery who sacrificed everything for freedom'. There is a trail of small stainless steel posts on either side of the path to the viewpoint, each listing a unit of the 2nd Canadian Corps, from armoured and infantry brigades to medical and signal corps, dental corps and postal and pay corps. It's fascinating to see the range of duties, skills and services needed to keep an army operational.

BRETTEVILLE-SUR-LAIZE CANADIAN CEMETERY (Rue du Prieuré/D167, just north of the junction with D183; 21km south of Caen; w veterans.gc.ca/eng/ remembrance/memorials/overseas/second-world-war/france/bretteville; ⅋) A

stone entrance with four classical porticos, flanked by the flags of France and Canada, leads you into this large cemetery on land conceded permanently to Canada by the French government. Here lie 2,958 men, of which 2,782 are Canadians, with 87 unidentified, plus 80 British, four Australians, one from France and one from New Zealand. Most of them were killed in July 1944 around Saint-André-sur-Orne and the battles around the Falaise Pocket. In the village of Bretteville-sur-Laize itself, look out for the street names: rue du Royal Black Watch and rue des Canadiens honour the companies that liberated the village. By the cemetery's main entrance, a stone memorial in the shape of a maple leaf bears the name Gerard Doré. At the age of 15 he joined Les Fusiliers Mont-Royal and was killed on 23 July, aged just 16.

POLISH WAR CEMETERY (Cimetière militaire polonais; junction of D131 & D658 near Urville; 25km south of Caen; ♿) This is the only Polish World War II cemetery in France, opened in October 1946. There are 696 graves, of which 615 came from the 1st Armoured Division (Polish Hussars), which suffered appalling losses in the battle to take Caen and then the Falaise Gap battles. The remaining graves are Polish soldiers who died elsewhere in France. A dramatic, V-shaped monument, with a stylised aluminium Polish eagle sculpture that gleams in the sunlight, dominates the cemetery. The graves run in neat rows, marked with a simple stone cross and brass plaque with the soldier's name, rank and date of death. As you walk out the gates, adorned with the insignia of the division, you are left with a very real sense of the Polish sacrifice.

EAST OF CAEN

HÉROUVILLE-SAINT-CLAIR Just outside Caen's ring road, on the wall of the Église Saint-Clair, a small plaque remembers 32 men of the British **2nd Battalion, Royal Lincolnshire Regiment**, who gave their lives liberating Hérouville-Saint-Clair on 8 July 1944, and the further 208 Lincolnshire soldiers who fell in France, Belgium, the Netherlands and Germany.

BANNEVILLE-LA-CAMPAGNE CWGC CEMETERY (On D675 by Sannerville, 8km east of Caen; ♿) This is a particularly peaceful cemetery, surrounded by farmland. There are 2,170 Commonwealth graves here, including five Australian, 11 Canadian and two New Zealanders, plus 140 unknown, as well as five Polish soldiers, whose gravestones feature a distinctive pointed arch. They were killed in the fighting between July – when Caen was captured – and August, when the Falaise Gap closed.

SAINT-DÉSIR-DE-LISIEUX This village, some 50km from Caen, has two war cemeteries next to each other, with a connecting memorial path between them: one is for German soldiers, the other for Allies (rue de la Libération, by junction of D159 & D613). This is the most easterly of the Normandy cemeteries, and the men buried here were killed mostly in the final stages of the Battle of Normandy, as the German forces that had escaped the Falaise Pocket (page 117), and the Allied troops pursuing them, raced to the crossings over the Lower Seine River. The **CWGC cemetery** (♿) contains 598 Commonwealth graves, of which 78 were brought from Chartres (Saint Chéron) communal cemetery after the war. Most of those buried in the **German cemetery** (w kriegsgraeberstaetten.volksbund.de/friedhof/st-desir-de-lisieux; ♿) died during a series of defensive battles along the River Touques. There are 3,735 dead, in three long blocks, and each red sandstone cross has the names of four fallen soldiers, two on each face.

Appendix 1

FURTHER READING

The D-Day landings and Normandy campaign must be one of the most written-about military events in modern history. There is no shortage of books to read, but you might look at:

Holland, James *Normandy '44* Bantam Press, 2019. Holland is probably the most authoritative World War II historian in recent years; his books are widely praised and respected. For a more granular perspective, his book *Brothers in Arms* (Penguin Random House, 2021) follows one tank regiment, the Sherwood Rangers Yeomanry, into Normandy and then on to Germany.

Marriott, Leo and Forty, Simon *The Normandy Battlefields – D-Day and the Bridgehead* Casemate Publishers, 2014. Amazingly detailed descriptions of the battlefields, stuffed full of maps and illustrations, historic and contemporary images and lots of aerial photographs. There is an excellent second volume, co-written with George Forty: *The Normandy Battlefields – Bocage and Breakout* Casemate Publishers, 2014.

Ryan, Cornelius *The Longest Day* Simon & Schuster, 1959. It's a little old now, but this was the original work on D-Day, and it's written like a thriller – even if you know how it ends! Of course it spawned the movie of the same name (page 24), which has gone on to inform most people's view of D-Day. Worth a read.

Sterne, Gary, *D-Day Cover-up at Pointe-du-Hoc* Pen & Sword Military, 2019. This is the detailed follow-up to Gary's first book, *The Cover-up at Omaha Beach*, which covers the mystery of the missing guns at Pointe-du-Hoc and the role of the nearby Maisy Battery.

There are also several publishers that produce a range of excellent books on D-Day, including:

Orep Editions (W orepeditions.com) This Bayeux-based publisher produces a wide range of books and booklets on Normandy in 1944, in multiple languages. Authoritatively written by French experts and historians, they often bring fresh insight, new detail and rare images. It's worth keeping an eye open for their books in museum shops in Normandy.

Pen & Sword (W pen-and-sword.co.uk) This specialist UK publisher offers many books covering World War II and Normandy. It has a series called Battleground Europe covering specific battles and campaigns in detail – a whole book to one battle.

Appendix 2

GLOSSARY

ARMY STRUCTURE Military units and formations are notoriously difficult to define. They can vary wildly in size, structure and purpose from one army to another and at different points in history. So definitions have to be broad, and there will always be exceptions.

Platoon	A unit made up of 25–30 soldiers, or 36 in the British Army. Platoons are commanded by a lieutenant or second lieutenant.
Company	A unit with roughly 100 to 250 men in two or more platoons, commanded by a captain or major.
Battalion	A unit with somewhere between 400 and 1,000 men in four or more companies, commanded by a lieutenant colonel.
Regiment	A core unit in most armies, commanded by a colonel. The regiment, often raised and recruited locally, is the 'family' unit for its soldiers. An infantry regiment would usually comprise two battalions, reaching about 800–1,000 men each, or eight to ten companies. A tank regiment would be smaller, with around 600–900 troopers and up to 72 tanks; tank regiments are divided into squadrons rather than battalions, and subdivided into troops or tank companies.
Brigade	A tactical military formation that would normally comprise two or three regiments, typically 2,500 men, plus supporting elements, such as artillery, engineers and logistics units. Two or three brigades may constitute a division, and they were typically commanded by a brigadier. They would be assembled for specific missions or functions, which could be long-running.
Division	A major formation of an army or corps. The size and structure of an army division in 1944 varied depending on the country and the type of division. However, most divisions were organised into two or three brigades. In addition to infantry units, the division might also include a number of support units such as artillery, engineers, signals, reconnaissance, medical and quartermaster units. The strength of an American infantry division in 1944 was approximately 15,000 men. German infantry divisions in 1944 were similarly structured, but they were typically smaller than American divisions, around 10,000 men. British infantry divisions were also structured into three brigades, with approximately 18,300 men.
Corps	A formation comprising two or more divisions with anywhere between 20,000 to 60,000 men, commanded by a general or possibly a lieutenant general.

Field Army	A 'command' – a collection of units and formations under the control of a single officer eg: a field marshal. It might comprise 100,000–200,000 men in two to four corps.

OTHER TERMINOLOGY

AA	Anti-aircraft defensive forces, such as guns and barrage balloons.
Advanced landing ground (ALG)	Makeshift airfields; see page 52 for further information.
AVRE	Armoured Vehicle Royal Engineers; see page 28 for further information.
Battery	A group of artillery guns operating together. This might be a group of mobile artillery field guns (howitzers) or, on the German side, a fixed emplacement of four or more large guns in reinforced casemates. Some of the German batteries had mobile field guns in fixed circular emplacements to complement the big guns, for example at the batteries at Crisbecq and Merville. Allied artillery batteries were all mobile, either towed or self-propelled (page 138).
Beach obstacles	In addition to artillery batteries inland, and fixed defences immediately behind a beach (Widerstandsnests, pillboxes, trenches, tobruks etc), the Atlantic Wall beaches themselves were covered, above and below the waterline, with obstacles. The most common were shallow-angled log ramps and leaning log posts, many with anti-tank mines attached, designed to stop, damage, tip up or explode landing craft. Steel barriers, called 'Belgian gates' because they looked like large gates, blocked the channels between other obstacles. Three steel girders welded together in a star shape, called 'hedgehogs', were designed to rip the bottom out of landing craft or block them when exposed, as were iron pyramid shapes covered in concrete, called 'tetrahydras'. The Allies had teams of demolition frogmen in the first assault wave, or ahead of it, whose job was to blow a path through these obstacles with explosives. It's fair to say they suffered a high casualty rate.
Blockhouse	(German: Blockhaus) A standalone fortification or observation post.
Bridgehead	A foothold, or strategically important area of ground around a sea or river landing site/crossing point. To 'establish a bridgehead' is to secure a landing ground that is no longer contested.
Casemate	A fortified enclosure or bunker from which large guns can be fired.
Command post (CP)	The in-the-field HQ for the commander of a unit.
Commando	A small military unit specially trained to make quick, surprise attacks.
Corvette	The smallest type of warship.
DD Tank	A Duplex Drive tank; the two drive systems being tracks and propellers. The DD tank was the swimming version of the Sherman tank with a tall canvas skirt that kept it afloat.
Destroyer	A fast, manoeuvrable, long-endurance warship mostly used as an escort vessel to protect other vessels from submarines and aircraft.
Draw	A gully or ravine, as in the Vierville Draw or Colleville Draw, which exit off Omaha Beach. There are dozens of different names for these topographical features – 'draw' is the US term, while if you came from Dorset, England, from where many soldiers embarked for D-Day, you might call it a 'chine'.

Enfilade	A unit is 'in enfilade' if the enemy can fire its weapons along its longest axis for maximum damage. Men in a trench are 'in defilade' if fire is coming in from the front, but 'in enfilade' if the enemy attacks from the side, firing along the length of the trench.
GIR	Glider Infantry Regiment. Airborne troops delivered by glider rather than parachute. Once down on the ground, their pilots became combat troops. The American-designed Waco could carry 13 troops, while the British Horsa could carry 25.
Landing craft	A range of landing craft at Normandy were used to deliver troops, weapons and supplies. The most well known are the American LCVP (Landing Craft Vehicle and Personnel), or 'Higgins boat' (named after its designer, Andrew Higgins), which could carry 36 soldiers with full kit. The British version was the LCA (Landing Craft Assault) which carried between 30 and 35. The US also had a larger LCI (Landing Craft Infantry) which could land 200 fully equipped troops. The US LCM (Landing Craft Mechanised) could take 60 soldiers or a 30-tonne tank, and their LST (Landing Ship Tank) could deliver 20 tanks or 400 equipped soldiers to the beach, while the British LCT (Landing Craft Tank) could carry three tanks. And there was the famous DUKW, the six-wheeled amphibious truck. Don't ask what it stood for. (Oh, OK. In the Ford Motor Company naming system: D = 1942 production series, U = utility, K = all-wheel drive, W = tandem rear axles, both driven. Well, you did ask!)
Pillbox	Small blockhouses, nicknamed 'pillboxes' because of their shape.
PIR	A Parachute Infantry Regiment. US airborne troops landed by parachute, not glider. Key units of the US 82nd and 101st airborne divisions. (The British had parachute brigades rather than regiments.)
Rangefinder	An optical device used to measure the distance to a target. It is essentially a long tube, rather like a double-ended periscope. The further apart the lenses at the ends of the tube – ie: the longer the tube is – the more accurate is the range.
Self-Propelled Guns (SPGs)	Tracked vehicles with thin armour on a tank chassis. The British Army named them after men of the cloth: Deacon, Priest, Sexton. The US Army gave them numbers: M7, M12, M40. The Sexton was the most common in Normandy.
Signal monuments	Nine memorials erected along the Normandy coast, designed by Yves-Marie Froidevaux, chief architect of the French National Historic Monuments, and built in 1949–50 with money from the scrapping of the Allied ships that remained on the Normandy beaches. They are meant to resemble the prow of a ship coming from the sea. There are also some quarter-size 'mini' signal monuments here and there.
Tobruk	A one-man bunker with a circular hole at the top, protecting most of the body, or all of it if the soldier ducked down inside. They were usually used for machine gunners, but a slightly larger two-man version could be used as a mortar position. Named after Tobruk in Libya, where they first appeared during the Siege of Tobruk in 1941.
Widerstandsnest (WN)	A 'resistance nest' or fortified German defensive position, sometimes also called a Stützpunkt (strongpoint). It might comprise one or more bunkers with large guns and other fixed defences such as barbed wire, trenches, minefields, and mortar and machine gun posts. They were numbered, eg: WN 27 in Saint-Aubin-sur-Mer.

Index

Page numbers in **bold** indicate major entries; those in *italics* indicate maps.

INDEX OF ADVERTISERS

NORMANDY WAY

Presented To You By

The World's Greatest Hike And Cycling Trails On One Platform

- This official Normandy Way is a verified 300km cycling loop;
- The Waytrails app will reliably navigate you as well as tell you what happened at over 60 checkpoints;
- Bespoke content created by historians and experts with additional archive images, stories and features;
- Explore the Normandy beaches, ancient Norman history and beautiful countryside that bring these places to life.

GET THE WAYTRAILS APP TO DISCOVER YOUR NORMANDY WAY

Plan your route, book your travel and hotels, add your activities, read the stories & navigate the official trail with confidence.

www.waytrails.com